Business Guides on the Go

"Business Guides on the Go" presents cutting-edge insights from practice on particular topics within the fields of business, management, and finance. Written by practitioners and experts in a concise and accessible form the series provides professionals with a general understanding and a first practical approach to latest developments in business strategy, leadership, operations, HR management, innovation and technology management, marketing or digitalization. Students of business administration or management will also benefit from these practical guides for their future occupation/careers.

These Guides suit the needs of today's fast reader.

Waldemar Schneider

Taoist Principles and Practices in Management

Success in a Multicultural Business

Waldemar Schneider
Walldorf, Germany

ISSN 2731-4758 ISSN 2731-4766 (electronic)
Business Guides on the Go
ISBN 978-3-031-31175-8 ISBN 978-3-031-31176-5 (eBook)
https://doi.org/10.1007/978-3-031-31176-5

© The Editor(s) (if applicable) and The Author(s), under exclusive license to Springer Nature Switzerland AG 2023

This work is subject to copyright. All rights are solely and exclusively licensed by the Publisher, whether the whole or part of the material is concerned, specifically the rights of translation, reprinting, reuse of illustrations, recitation, broadcasting, reproduction on microfilms or in any other physical way, and transmission or information storage and retrieval, electronic adaptation, computer software, or by similar or dissimilar methodology now known or hereafter developed.
The use of general descriptive names, registered names, trademarks, service marks, etc. in this publication does not imply, even in the absence of a specific statement, that such names are exempt from the relevant protective laws and regulations and therefore free for general use.
The publisher, the authors, and the editors are safe to assume that the advice and information in this book are believed to be true and accurate at the date of publication. Neither the publisher nor the authors or the editors give a warranty, expressed or implied, with respect to the material contained herein or for any errors or omissions that may have been made. The publisher remains neutral with regard to jurisdictional claims in published maps and institutional affiliations.

This Springer imprint is published by the registered company Springer Nature Switzerland AG
The registered company address is: Gewerbestrasse 11, 6330 Cham, Switzerland

This treatise contains selected translations for the profound verses of the classic *Tao Te Ching* composition incl. verses 7, 12, 49, 57, 60, 63, 79 captured from www.tao-te-king.org; verses 2, 15, 33 rendered by Wing-Tsit Chan; verses 5, 6, 8, 9, 11, 14, 20, 28, 30, 34, 36, 38, 39, 40, 48, 55, 56, 61, 67 deduced by Stephen Mitchell (thetaoteching.com); verses 1, 4, 10, 13, 18, 26, 27, 29, 35, 41, 46, 62, 66, 70, 77, 80, 81 transferred by Thomas Cleary; verses 23, 24, 44, 54, 71, 73 converted by Robert G. Henricks; verses 3, 16, 17, 19, 21, 22, 25, 32, 42, 43, 45, 47, 53, 58, 59, 64, 68, 69, 74, 78 decoded by J. H. McDonald, and verses 37, 51, 52, 75 deciphered by John C. H. Wu—among the best known interpretations.

Acknowledgements

My thanks are directed toward Ansgar Gerstner, whose book *The Tao of Business* has inspired initial considerations for this treatise.

Distinctive gratitude goes to Phillip Beniac, as a truly gifted leader enthusiastic about creating strategies and building confidence in the exploration of developing markets. Key insights into the playing field of the global competition were provided by Marco Burkhardt. As an open-minded interlocutor, Thomas Goettsche has provided valuable advice on Chinese expressions. Proofreading and encouragement from Samantha Wong have secured focus on the improvements within the transcription process.

Ongoing efforts of the "Success Across"[1] team continuously provide vividness for collaboration in multinational settings.

All the staff at Springer Nature publishing house were very helpful, with great care and a keen sense of quality. My particular appreciation goes to Barbara Bethke for her support with this publication.

---

[1] Follow their website successacross.com/en.

Key Terms

Taoism is a philosophical tradition of Chinese origin, which outlines the essential postulates of existence. ***Tao*** 道 ("*The Way*") represents fundamental principles as the substance of everything that can exist. ***Te*** 德 translated as *virtue* or *power* can be viewed as substantiation of these principles. Its basic virtues refer to sense *jīngshén* with ***jīng*** 精 often translated as essence, and ***shén*** 神 as an inclusive mind.

Tao Te Ching 道德经 (TTC) is a compilation of 81 aphorisms providing concise observations with insights into a general truth.[1]

Héxié 和谐 stands for "*harmony*" as combination of an attainment achieved by adaptation to the ongoing changes.

Qì 气 by the means of "*vital energy field*" cultivation causes the passive and active dynamics of ***yīn*** 阴 and ***yáng*** 阳 combination of later represents the evolving cycle of opposite polarities, which can be brought to harmony through balance.

---

[1] It has been translated more often than any other work (except the *Bible*).

Wújí 无极 implies "*everlasting*" or "*unbounded*" in writings of Chinese logicians, meant as being situated before the differentiation between an inactivity and motion.

Wúwéi 无为 is a key concept meaning "*non-interference*" or genuine "*effortless action.*"

Zirán 自然 as dynamic self-organization is regarded as a central value in Taoism.

For further meaning of these terms, see entries in https://www.en.wikipedia.org.

Contents

Introduction	1
Leading Principles	7
Balance of Power	15
Applications and Implications	
TAO and *TE* as Unity in Diversity	25
Wújí Within the Company Values	43
Wúwéi in the Management of Affairs	53
Zìrán in the Course of Events	67
Qì in Cyclic Innovation	79
Jìng in Dynamic Adaptation	91
Shen in the Sense of Community	107
Héxié Within Globalization	125
Appendix	145

About the Author

Waldemar Schneider is an accomplished business development manager with analytical and strategic thinking who gained confidence in performing at international software and services organizations. During 25 years in service, he has acquired multicultural market experience at various country, regional, and international positions at IBM, SAS Institute, SAP, and InterComponentWare AG—an international healthcare company. In doing so, he learned to apply the *Taoist* principles with the consideration of integrative aspects and particularities of different communities in a changing business world.

Introduction

The classical *Taoism*[1] is a philosophical tradition of Chinese origin. It is based on the *Tao Te Ching* (TTC) containing 81 rather brief verses attributed to the sage *Lǎozǐ* ("*Old Master*" 老子 from the sixth century BCE). Each verse provides condensed insights into the principles of a complex reality, with indicated guidelines on appropriate efforts. The collection of concise Taoist statements indicates inner coherence with fundamental forces (*TAO*) that can manifest in any appearances according to the changing circumstances (*TE*). It is also perceived as "*inner power*" embodied in various individuals. Chinese *logograms* bear the ability to conceptualize complex ideas of an ongoing change in a condensed pictorial manner. Therefore, illustrations translated into scenes known to our cultural foundation have been well thought out.

This treatise combines key themes of Taoism, compiled for international managers who are on their way to become trusted leaders. Provided observations can empower readers to enrich their competencies

---

[1] Terms in *italic* are further explicated in https://en.wikipedia.org/wiki/.

coping with new situations. Following a short sketch of the leading principles, there is an overview of organizational themes. We will then review an application of selected doctrines enriched with insights by the narratives from suitable references and fitting TTC verses that imply assured value to leaders. *Taoist leaders* clearly possess genuine attention in the handling of any affairs in steady acting with discretion and foresight. Each distinct yet coherent Taoist principle gets applied for the study of its meaning within different business environments. If appropriate, case studies introduce further relevant details, for managers to contemplate on embedded examples for further aspirations. Bold readers are always encouraged to merge personal experience with the meaning of the Taoist insights for improvements in the multicultural business life.

Tao Te Ching shall be among primary sources for examination of its perceived influence with extended experience from the current business world. Most of the verses therein are addressing particularities of leadership impetus with flexibility in handling issues, and efficiency under challenging circumstances. They can provide insights into pragmatic treatment of situations within long-term strategic thinking based on situational awareness and managerial transformational abilities. Taoist tradition has been officially recognized by the People's Republic of China (PRC), is well known across Southeast Asia, and is partly applied around the world. Most of the methods common in the Western hemisphere are examined in China for their suitability and, if necessary, adjusted. Integrative value is highly rated across Southeast Asian companies that look for harmony in readiness to accept a compromise with the prospect of long-term gains.

We all write a life story under a variety of influences. Any and every successful global player tends to operate less in hierarchical orders and more in networking relations within relevant associations and in close contact with affiliates. The hierarchical decision-making structure is dominated by control, and the network-like consists of linkage and leads to cooperation. To prevail with shared goals and objectives, a common understanding of defined and agreed strategies is required. There are numerous books on collaborative leadership and innovative management based on Western insights and selected case studies—among quite popular are "The Leadership Challenge" by Kouzes and Posner, and "The

7 Habits of Highly Effective People" by Stephen R. Covey. However, none of them—with exception to "The Tao of Business" by Ansgar Gerstner—are reflections on the savvy wisdom of classical Taoism, which advocates expansion of self-awareness within broader society in a harmonious relationship toward sustainable development—it can be even expected to contribute to improved business performance with personal well-being, as it has been outlined in the publication "The Tao of Warren Buffett."

The following insights aim at helpful hints for success in business life, under consideration that every seed can grow into a plant providing favorable conditions. The terms *leadership* and *management* came to be a commonplace within business circles—striking, though, that their meaning differs substantially across various enterprises, as well as between Western and Eastern corporations. Let's see if leadership effectiveness is an innate skill. Or is it something that can be gained over time and experience? Foremost, we can state that leaders provide a renewed vision of what could be obtained, with a notion of animating values. In turn, managers can address the needs of their teams in the currency that most matters to them—in line with the corporate objectives. Regarding the all-encompassing Taoism, this composition is looking at leadership abilities and managerial capabilities as considerations that are particularly required for the overall growth from business in emerging markets with significant economic growth. Stability and change, as well as management and leadership, are interdependent and could be "*balanced*" or not. At best, excellent leaders and proficient managers can combine opposite approaches in a truly holistic way. They know how to make the use of available circumstances, without any embellishment or exaggeration.

Lasting development of a corporation can be attributed to effective leadership setting the course toward successful management. Striving to achieve top performance as a manager and leader, one shall always continuously execute deliberate practice in overcoming upcoming obstacles for sustainable business. *Leadership* in its essence continues to remain a contested concept with disputable facets to its appearances. Way back, Taoism has outlined certain critical behavior patterns of leadership traits. As being stated by John Heider, "*Tao Te Ching persuasively unites leadership skills and the leader's way of life*" (Heider 2015, p. xi). It is unequivocal that only by sharpening responsive insights we can fully realize own capacities in managing people and affairs in association with fundamental principles.

Further rehearsal of managerial abilities is going to give an edge to a vivid mind for realization of useful concepts—as the meaning of the verses in TTC can be applied in any context to restore for optimum efficiency, while their broader application is truly universal.

As discussed below, creative thinkers must find a balance between the established processes and assess the degree of chances from any innovative approaches. Always consider where we are rooted and what connections are there. Among other factors, potentiality and actuality play a role in business. Motivating others is a reciprocal habit.

The verse 21 of TTC *Lǎozǐ* has described how processes of ideation to realization build on each other with creation that comes from a fruitful ordinance of insight and intuition. Based on reflection from attentive analysis of influencing factors, personal *informed intuition* can be a great asset for any desirable attainment.

> *The greatest virtue you can have*
> *comes from following only the Tao;*
> *which takes a form that is intangible and evasive.*
> *Even though the Tao is intangible and evasive,*
> *we are able to know it exists.*
> *Intangible and evasive, yet it has a manifestation.*
> *Secluded and dark, yet there is a vitality within it.*
> *Its vitality is very genuine. Within it we can find order.*
> *Since the beginning of time, the Tao has always existed.*
> *It is beyond existing and not existing.*
> *How do I know where creation comes from?*
> *I look inside myself and see it.*

As further stated by John Heider "*There is no substitute for knowing how things happen and for acting accordingly*" (Heider, 2015, p. 21). *TAO* is representing enduring laws of natural forces that are causing instantiations (*TE*) according to the current conditions. When dealing with the complexity of the ever-changing reality, we are often challenged to see how to cope with it, and often there is a need to cut through a knot of Gordian proportions.

We are often concerned with disparity between the dynamics of disruptive development and continuous strive for stability. Taoist principles are laid on fair competition, free markets, and acknowledgment of individual contributions—all intertwined as a coherent worldview. Instead of accentuating on certain differences, these factors are laid on the *integrative thinking* in mind. The most recent innovations go along with *digital transformation*. Digitalization is a structural ingredient for systemic shift within organizations. Next to it is exploration of well-established processes so that they can be mirrored as a *digital twin* with modular characteristics. Just as important is the willingness to accept new impulses and adaptation of behavior to the changing conditions. The potential for any improved decision-making goes along a series of developmental steps. It can be observed that in the digital era an increasing number of data analysts gets recruited, while availability of statisticians that are trained to apply complex mathematical modeling is declining.

Digital transformation is not purely an advancement of computer-based technologies, and it radically involves process-driven social disruption with new demands across all areas. Seeking fulfillment from innovative ideas, it is influencing progressive developments in the economy as well as social life. This sometimes necessitates leaving behind well-known processes in favor of relatively new practices that are still being defined or refined.

With the increasing numbers of managers at different levels, many organizations often lack differentiating leaders. This does not mean that in transition to a new normal, we always need someone at the caliber of Steve Jobs or Elon Musk. Some modern entrepreneurs could successfully bring their start-up companies to reach impressive heights when leading into new areas of the twenty-first century. It's worth to explore skills and capabilities that unravel increasing complexity of the business world in appropriate manners. Contrary to well-established management practices, it is a multi-factored topic, which can get even more challenging in cross-cultural situations.

Accelerated business transformation creates sublime challenges in organizations. Within fast-changing environments, we can appreciate flexibility in thinking. The decision-making at any level requires agile and creative abilities. In its fundamental meaning, leadership is about a systematic way of exposing major targets combined with the continuous execution along the prime principles. The fervent desire to continuously work on improvements surely helps to add real value to the managerial objectives for improved proceeds in core business.

Ongoing technological diffusion contributes to overall reconciliation of economic and social objectives. With further convergence of financial and technological developments, we shall consider symptoms of *Chimerica* as symbolic postures of modern China and the US covering up to a third of global economic output. Increased collaboration across global enterprises in a creative synthesis of modern Western aspirations and ancient Chinese concepts leads to improved cooperation across boundaries towards common foundation. Certain American meritocracy could bring adversarial effects when applied within a Chinese context, as conveyed to some point below. As a high uncertainty avoidance country, Chinese business partners are less tolerant of ambiguity. Greater China has demonstrated impressive economic growth from improvements in infrastructure and technology, besides the logistics and labor management. It has opened to the inception of excellent products, proven expertise, and systems know-how by looking for improvements under given conditions. While Western advance often lies in the orientation on relationships behind appearances, principal interests in Eastern cultures often stand in the cultivation of harmonious relationships within social ambiance.

Taoism lays claim to gregarious execution starting from the idea of inner unity that is in unison with outward diversity grounded in the long-term benefits rather than short-term gains in a complex reality. How to gain value-based leadership skills? Let's explore its leading principles and manifold ways of balancing their appearances.

Leading Principles

We all are experiencing changes in the "*New Way of Working*" that calls for joint efforts toward "*collective outcome.*" The purpose-driven organizations are structured upon their destined understanding of internal and external processes, so that profitable growth is set on balanced amalgam of motivational leadership with skilled management. Successful leadership is based on effective principles, although their implementation allows for many variations. At an inflection point, leaders better be able to inspire high performance, while able managers adapt and drive change by bringing defined strategy to life.

In different parts of our polycentric world, people tend to comply with a variety of business customs that are often culturally linked to disparate approaches. For instance, in Germany, each business opportunity tends to be examined in greater detail within intensive discussions. Only by reaching an agreement, the process then moves toward the established objectives. In France, decisions are made hierarchically, reflecting mutual respect. Russian corporations adhere to a formal negotiation process, often followed by socializing events in case one succeeds. In Greater China, one needs to contemplate certain socially conservative values—chiefly the Chinese do not discuss business dealings while dining considering the *miànzi* 面子 concept of *"social standing"*[1] that plays an important role in the fabric of society. Business corporations are embedded into society. Within Southeast Asia, where many large corporations exhibit the traits of a community, an autocratic leadership, and paternalistic management style prevails—hence, any business appointments are to be set up well in advance. A rather short country visit may be perceived as an affront. Several trips there may be required, up to receiving confirmation for a desired meeting with the decision-maker or a major stakeholder.

The definition of leadership widely accepted in the Western Hemisphere was given by Martin M. Chemers as "*a process of social influence in which a person can enlist the aid and support of others in the accomplishment of a common task.*" The American psychologist Daniel Goleman even differentiates several leadership styles, such as affiliative, coaching, pacesetting, democratic, commanding, or visionary. A Chinese version of the leadership has been expressed by Xuezhi Guo "*The Mandate of Heaven implies that the legitimacy of political leadership as well as its leading figures come from not only their political power derived from their positions and* de facto *dominance in the leadership but also their roles in bringing voluntary compliance from the high-ranking leaders and the population at large*" (Guo 2019, p. 139). Taoism clearly upholds any open-minded manager by offering a flexible approach when dealing with circumstances in any dynamic environment under ever-changing conditions.

Leadership approaches and management styles can discreetly vary, but there are some fundamental practices that may apply in all cases. Leaders are usually capable of creating new contexts from fragmentary perceptions of reality, and they might have an aversion against idealistic actions. In turn, the successful managers are always in a standby mode for implementation of practical solutions. As described by Kouzes and Posner, any exemplary leaders are following the five practices "*Model the Way, Inspire a Shared Vision, Challenge the Process, Enable Others to Act, and Encourage the Heart*",[2] which—as the authors claim—have remained valid for over 40 years. In addition, they highlight expected credibility in

---

[1] "*Face*" by the meaning of self-respect and reputation, prestige, or honor.
[2] See a sketch on https://www.leadershipchallenge.com/Research/Five-Practices.aspx.

execution by stating, "*Leadership is not about who you are; it's about what you do.*"—suggesting as a seamless transition into effective management skills. Bypassing a certain threshold requires a change from informal and motivational leadership to structured and regulatory management.

While managers prefer evidence-based action, most leaders are also capable of precursive effects. According to several studies,[3] among most important commandments of an effective *Management* are

- coping with complexity through efficiency in solving problems
- constantly implementing organizational skills and structure
- defining targets and deadlines in human-related processes
- focusing on transformation execution (tracking progress)
- concentrating on clarity and accuracy in communication.

In a best-possible combination, they can be paired with the pivotal qualities of enabling *Leadership*, such as

- curiosity and inspiring imagination in coping with change
- ability to take on challenges by creating solutions
- ability to grasp the innovator's paradox
- credibility with convincing visions
- shaping change outcomes.

Management at different levels of a business is a complex discipline of personal and collaborative organizational activities in the best-possible supervising manner. It is focusing on operational excellence that is considerate to secure growth with expected high yields under favorable conditions, as well as securing a stable position under given circumstances. Managerial competence combines skills with attitudes. Effective managers can largely nourish intrinsic activities, ensuring incubation of strengthened beliefs through joint reflection. Have you tried to see how long it takes to turn beliefs into behaviors? Rather than accepting a vague "*it depends,*" it is better to take into consideration the striking

---

[3] See https://keydifferences.com/difference-between-leader-and-manager.html.

method developed by the *Lefkoe Institute*[4] in view that increasing competency enables flexibility in judgment and supports situational fluency by considering emotional merits that can help one successfully collaborate with others.

In its fundamental way, leadership is about a systematic way of exposing major targets in combination with continuous execution along the prime principles. A clear sign of maturity is the ability to perceive contradictions, especially when dealing within different cultural states of affairs. Practical knowledge is based on the reflected experience. By reviewing the verses of TTC, we shall note that its theme of a "*harmonious leadership*" has been grounded in a persistent belief that a honest leader (resp. *sage*) is persistently applying durable principles (of *TAO*) from experience and insights into socially requisite ideals (as *TE*). The mindset that is formed by the *yin and yang* duality framework can reflect varying aspects of the same system within cyclical development patterns. An agile company is in a steady flow. Decision-making at any level requires agile and creative mediative abilities. Many decisions are made according to cultural differences or with respect to different values. Only by identifying correlating business concepts and adapting them to overall enterprise objectives, one can add value to the new revenue opportunities. In relation to fast-changing environments, we need flexibility in thinking. The verse 28 in TTC shows combining polarity of doing and being.

> *Know the male, yet keep to the female:*
> *receive the world in your arms.*
> *If you receive the world, the Tao will never leave you*
> *and you will be like a little child.*
> *Know the white, yet keep to the black:*
> *be a pattern for the world.*
> *If you are a pattern for the world, the Tao will be strong inside you*
> *and there will be nothing you can't do.*
> *Know the personal, yet keep to the impersonal:*
> *accept the world as it is.*
> *If you accept the world, the Tao will be luminous inside you*

---

[4] Incl. blog and offerings on www.mortylefkoe.com.

> *and you will return to your primal self.*
> *The world is formed from the void, like utensils from a block of wood.*
> *The Master knows the utensils, yet keeps to the block:*
> *thus she can use all things.*

The first three paragraphs follow the pattern *know—keep—be* held by collation in pairs of striking terms with a reference to a common base. To craft a role model for constituents, the *master* preserves harmonious development by securing impartial balance of compelling *simplicity*. Hence, she does not lead being possessive through sophisticated knowledge, but by underlying candor when advising in undemanding fashion with tolerance to any possible deviations omitting expendable interventions. Extremes complement each other, avoiding compulsiveness. The way of *doing the right thing* while doing the things right is best preserved for an interplay of emerging leadership that is skillful interlinked with thorough management.

Chinese way of introducing change is never fundamentally disturbing, as thrill from short-lived success cannot sustain against set views and habits. In Greater China, this is called *guānxi* 关系—a term that defines the culture of honoring contractual obligations while reducing dysfunctional behavior under fundamental dynamics within networks of power. This concept of cohesion in economic relationships has survived decades of Maoist doctrine. A network of personal connections still has major influence on the management of businesses owned by Chinese in Southeast Asia, favoring a *contingency leadership* style. It can be observed that the size of a company's network is highly correlated to their efficiency. Inclusion of contingency measures heightens flexibility. By considering self-disclosure and proving respect, assertion business relationships can be strengthened so that mutual success gets consolidated by the means of reciprocity. In the Western hemisphere, this has been rather seen with caution.[5]

Fruitful cooperation relies on the awareness of common goals. True compassion results from clear understanding of objectives. Being in line with reproducible strategies, a truly sound plan of actions is embedded into context of current position and prevalent tendencies.

---

[5] See https://en.wikipedia.org/wiki/Guanxi#In_a_business_context.

Within the decentralized corporation structures, there is an increasing demand to empower staff for purpose in their work. Servant leaders prefer to put organization ahead of themselves. Their ability to inspire conviction with modesty and awaken raising aspirations among their followers is an extraordinary gift. It's a managerial task though to take care of their subordinates in weighing up the promising options at stake and arrive at a sensible choice, keeping the needs and benefits of clients the foremost considerations.

Both the *servant leadership* and Taoism approaches are based on self-awareness, sense of humbleness, and faith on joint future. Trust accelerates processes. In a dispute of structure and system, the verse 49 of TTC emphasizes necessity in faithfulness with open mindset especially when dealing with all kinds of contradictions.

> *The **wise men** have **no fixed ambition**,*
> *so, they **make others' aims** their **vision**.*
> *To **good men**, **I am good**, to **men***
> *that are **not good**, **I'm good again**:*
> *to **get** the most of **goodness** then!*
> *To **true men**, **I am true**, to **men***
> *that are **not true**, **I'm true again**:*
> *most **faithfulness attaining** then!*
> ***Amidst the world** the **wise men stay**,*
> *to **act there** in **a humble way**,*
> *their **heart-felt aims: not fixed** are they.*
> ***All other people** seek advice*
> *and **fix** to them **their ears** and **eyes** –*
> ***they all** are **children to** the **wise** ...*

In Chinese texts, *virtue* was closely linked to *servant leadership* as a promoter of differential goal attainment. Completeness can arise from integration according to the rules of the game of unity in diversity.[6] Acting with integrity in a complex world, the evolving leaders know well-available abilities with an openness to any obstacles.

The scale and pace of the changes taking place in Central and Southeast Asia are extraordinary. Chinese leaders shall know best the meaning

---

[6] Motto in my book on "Reflections on the Taoist worldview" ("Reflektionen auf das Taoistische Weltbild" in German).

of "*coping with change.*" Certain activities can only be done at the expense of others. Which of the perceived options could get you to a balanced reward? By leading without violating the natural flow of things, top executives could consider alternative behaviors through anticipated effects. Presently, many Asian businesses are open to follow new ideas with experimentation. They are ready to apply different perspectives, and chart-optimized courses. In the strong tailwind of Singapore with success in Taiwan and South Korea, there are growing moves in Vietnam, Malaysia, and Indonesia. Limitations arise from preconceived notions. Sometimes, TTC refers to distinctive features of a "*Sage*," as in the verse 2 of TTC

> *... the Sage manages affairs without action*
> *and spreads doctrine without words.*
> *All things arise, and he does not turn away from them.*
> *He produces them but does not take possession of them.*
> *He acts but does not rely on his own ability.*
> *He accomplishes his task but does not claim credit for it.*
> *It is precisely because he does not claim credit*
> *that his accomplishment remains with him.*

Nowadays, such abilities can be expected from a senior executive or a high caliber mentor within or outside the model organization. They show by model, avoid disturbing interventions, and convince by composed modesty with qualities of tolerance for mistakes, proficiency in absolute assessment of critical liminal spaces, and forward-looking attitude by mastering any unexpected obstacles.

When building distinctive competences, the boundary-crossing processes demand an understanding of underlying dynamics. Appreciating diversity, an ongoing unwavering commitment shall support inclusive and equitable societies. New conditions can arise from occurred obstacles. One can address them with sincere respect to expertise and thorough commitment to affected peers and counterparts.

Reality is quite complex, and change is ever constant. There is never a final stage in an iterative process to render a given structure, in which several parties are involved. Leaders benefit from self-esteem and time and again get asked to fill in a prestigious position. They are surrounded by managers that want to increase their chances of being promoted to the top of their line of business by pursuing declared objectives rigorously. An inspiring leader is distinguished by a creative will to shape things. Although new perspectives are mostly based on own and adopted experiences, a Taoist leader knows well how to remain unbiased and to emphasize the attainment of balance by the means of moderation in simplicity. Even small changes can have a big impact. Great leader understands impact, creates consensus, and aligns talent toward workable solutions.

Accelerated transformation creates sublime challenges in organizations. Greater China was already the largest economy in fifteenth and eighteenth centuries and is about to become so again in the current one. There are some subtle elements in the business culture within China worth to be aware of where elaborated forms of decision-making delineate the limits of organizational processes in their own established ways. Leaders can become moderators of decision-making processes. When conducting negotiations there, one should always provide a wholistic perspective on the overall values from your offering. It can be perceived as peculiar to focus on specific topics of the agreement, such as certain conditions, that destruct from main clauses.

This treatise is structured along major concepts of classical Taoism, emphasizing key faculties of sound leadership paired with effective management. Taoist view on leadership emanates from an ongoing engagement with the natural order according to the insights into given circumstances. Leaders of this ilk are influential because they "*walk the talk*" by understanding and respecting self, others, process, and the system. Being well connected within the "*power base*," they can maintain integrity with the common base.

Balance of Power

Global businesses are exposed to insecurities. *Harmonization* is an ongoing effort for global economic players, ensuring that contributions across different lines of business result in a coherent set of implementation guidelines. Every corporation is considerably interconnected through co-operation with other companies, incl. relationship with their alliances and suppliers, with whom top management takes efforts in establishing joint values. Which errands can bring you off-track? When getting out of sync, see if underlying forces can get you going in the expected direction. Don't let your considerations to get distant from the actuality of experience. Balance and harmony are among the main perspectives that have formed this discourse.

It pays off to strive for the vigilant understanding of the fundamental powers that are driving change. Many virtues expressed in the verses of TTC promote certain attitudes, which enable prosperous business ventures within dynamic markets, as stated in the verse 42 of TTC

> *The Tao gave birth to One. The One gave birth to Two.*
> *The Two gave birth to Three.*
> *The Three gave birth to all of creation.*

> *All things carry Yin yet embrace Yang.*
> *They blend their life breaths in order to produce harmony.*
> *People despise being orphaned, widowed and poor.*
> *But the noble ones take these as their titles.*
> *In loosing much is gained, and in gaining much is lost.*
> *What others teach I too will teach:*
> *"The strong and violent will not die a natural death."*

An incremental expansion from natural development can be viewed by differentiation of business models.[1] Creative interaction emerges from mastering polarities within any unfolding opportunities of ongoing development. Several attributions of *yáng* can be assigned to leadership, while some associated with *yīn* can be reflected by managerial habits. Hence, we reflect their interrelation toward consensus and stability with the well-known *yin and yang* symbol at the front of each chapter.

Humanity has experienced that *multipolarity* is more stable and conflict-prone than *bipolar systems*. Tension usually arises when there are multiple claimants to a particular asset, so one needs to be aware of the limitations on the proper use of available supplies. Taking into account communication effort and coordination costs, an orchestrated use of global resources contributes to operational efficiency. Attention to cultural effectiveness pays off in creating a winning strategy. The intended meaning of terms such as business *proposal*, *obligation*, *performance*, *teamwork*, and *acceptance clause* can differ depending on valid regulations. But only mutual support by sharing individual strengths and supplementing limiting weaknesses leads to win–win situations. People tend to look after their intrinsic interests when forming groups, as described in the chapter "***TAO*** and ***TE*** as Unity in Diversity" where we review facets of leadership under multiple considerations of workplace conditions.

Classical Taoism arose during the *Warring States period*, characterized by warfare and consolidation of legislative reforms. As such, the dynamic relationship between individual and society got in the focus of considerations within TTC, which has compiled prudent advices for best-possible deployment of conditions that can be applied to improving

---

[1] https://businessmodelzoo.com/business-models/multi-sided-business-model.

efficiency of organizations. Openness and inclusiveness as advocated in the *sustainability* concept can have an impact on the organizational productivity. Let's review how these doctrines enable efficiency of exemplary organizations in the chapter "***Wújí*** within Company Values."

British parliament introduced the precautionary principle of "*checks and balances*" for the distribution of good governmental powers, meaning that while the ruler was *de jure* in charge, he was de facto obliged to reach consent with his ministers who were controlled by the Houses of Parliament. This might as well be viewed as a business-like transaction, as it shows a web of mutual dependence. *John Locke* (1632–1704) has argued in 1690 in "Two Treaties of Government" that drawing on responsibilities in the ancient idea of a "*natural law*" people could confer executive power on higher ranks with their obligation to protect common rights as defined within the "*Bill of Rights 1689.*" In that regard, one of the main Taoist principles has been delineated in the chapter "***Wúwéi*** in the Management of Affairs."

Dependable leadership effectiveness does not restrict spaces of action in their networks—they aim at bringing out the best in the team members. Such faculties combine intentional guidance and influence for greater achievements. The verse 17 of TTC is exhibiting leadership guidance by the means of subtle influence.

> *The best leaders are those the people hardly know exist.*
> *The next best is a leader who is loved and praised.*
> *Next comes the one who is feared.*
> *The worst one is the leader that is despised.*
> *If you don't trust the people, they will become untrustworthy.*
> *The best leaders value their words and use them sparingly.*
> *When she has accomplished her task,*
> *the people say, "Amazing: we did it, all by ourselves!".*

Taoism encourages leadership by empowerment. Best leaders don't force their insights into the foreground. Roger T. Ames pointed out that "*the minimum amount of external interference projected onto the individual from those in power, combined with an environment most conductive with the individual's quest for personal fulfillment."*[2]

A key point of trust comes down to delivering on any promises being stated, although unexpected situations can be around the corner, as sketched in the chapter "***Zirán*** in the Course of Events."

We surely know that an understanding of a broad and coherent strategic perspective at different levels of conditions in local legislation, regional market development, and global trends is beneficial. Adherence to corporate regulations is expected with unrestricted flow of *Qi* for unification in the field of business. We need to acknowledge that management of human resources is part of the whole, and as such cannot bear sole responsibility for success or failure. Responsibility assumed voluntarily is only partially related to the assigned duties based on the position or function. The long-term success depends on product quality and service reliability, but also on the flexibility of partners and suppliers. Layers of responsibility turn up on any extent: personal (commitment to promises), professional (contractual obligations), or even corporate (shared efforts toward company's vision and mission). Insightful commitment to common goals by all employees is required for a smooth development of the corporation. They contribute to continuous transformation, as has been propagated in the chapter "***Qi*** in Cyclic Innovation."

Any given situations are of a temporary nature since our social environment is in a constant interchange and whatever is in place now can quickly change. Most people prefer execution of any reasonable activities rather than following rigid rules in processes, which aim at disturbing effects. Hence, an agile manager will get committed to the results with increasing level of *empowerment*. Within ambitious business transformation processes, a competent leader with the Taoist mindset will unremittingly pay attention to non-intervention when new communities are unfolding and avoid *fundamental attribution error*, appreciating non-interference of diversity and variety in processes of self-organization as expressed in the verse 29 of TTC

---

[2] Quote from p. 41 in Roger T. Ames "The Art of Rulership: *A Study of Ancient Chinese Political Thought*" (1994).

Balance of Power

> *Should you want to take the world and contrive to do so.*
> *I see you won't manage to finish.*
> *The most sublime instrument in the world cannot be contrived.*
> *Those who contrive spoil it; those who cling lose it.*

In the translation of Wing-tsit Chan, we receive herewith a word of caution to the process state that runs the risk of being out of balance.

> *Therefore the sage discards the extremes,*
> *the extravagant and the excessive.*

If a process develops to an extreme state, it can transform into its opposite. For a coherent conduct of the *risk assessment*, it is worth to thoroughly review driving forces taking into consideration topics around *being* and *doing*, that are partly addressed in the chapter "**Jing** in Dynamic Adaptation."

Any society is based on multi-cultural influences. The restriction to development in one's own country limits the degree of effectiveness and can be associated with higher costs. It is crucial to consider what issues matter for courageous decisions in other parts of the world. We can learn how workability best combines insight with flexibility, as being traced with the important points to note within the chapter "**Shen** in the Sense of Community."

The disruptive nature of technological paradigm shifts can have severe implications for the corporate game plans. With increased uncertainty from constantly changing conditions, any proven strategies might become less viable. To what extent are the desired activities in line with the economic development in the world that we are shaping? For the ongoing implementation of balanced concepts, it is essential to detect and apply best practices within structural frameworks. Utilizing foresight abilities, leaders can perceive key processes as a coherent whole and aid in defeat of concerns, as outlined in the chapter "**Héxié** within Globalization."

It's a commonplace that business life is interrelated and dynamic. Less known is how to achieve efficiency within scalable growth. Post-globalization could bring a greater flexibility due to the ability to react more quickly in the competition for scarce resources. Independence from monopolies makes it easier to isolate the problem areas. Coordinated leadership involves understanding of the related organizations and continuous observation of significant conditions.

While this treatise is based on overall experience at certain leadership styles and management functions proven as long-term success with conformity to the Taoist principles, some embedded case studies are complementary and used as an illustration for the points made. Many organizations aim at applying a portfolio of proven *best practices*—sometimes radical,[3] more often incremental–to best match goals with realities. Herewith, desirable performance can be increased by concentrating resources on the essential issues, especially when the planning focus is on tasks with the greatest possible lifting power.

Following this introduction, we come to the overview of the topics that are essential for the application of Taoist principles in business. Of particular interest in each chapter, below is a notion of leadership embracing change, with implications for management exemplified with occurrences in different cultural geographies.

---

[3] Derived from the Latin *radix*, meaning "change at the root".

Applications and Implications

At all times, there are no downright certainties. Even if all preconditions from an ongoing assessment make an appearance, at any instance further intermediaries could turn up, hindering advancement. Remarkably, the research conducted by Harvard Business Review (HBR) has revealed that "*outstanding performance is the product of years of deliberate practice and coaching, not of any innate talent or skill.*" With "Paradox in harmony,"[1] Emmet McElhatton and Brad Jackson have reviewed various Chinese models. They declare that "*Tao helps the leader to conceptually reconcile opposites towards strategic and ethical ends.*" and arrive at a judgment by reasoning "*Thus the harmonious leader avoids ideologies of 'boxed-in' though, wields authority within being authoritarian, prefers peace but is decisive in war, and has a toolbox of hard (transactional), soft (inspirational) and smart skills that can be utilized according to context.*" Likewise, the verse 25 of TTC outlines the inexhaustible origins:

Before the universe was born
there was something in the chaos of the heavens.
It stands alone and empty, solitary and unchanging.
It is ever present and secure.

---

[1] journals.sagepub.com/doi/abs/10.1177/1742715012444054 (references).

It may be regarded as the Mother of the universe.
Because I do not know its name, I call it the Tao.
If forced to give it a name, I would call it 'Great'.
Because it is Great means it is everywhere.
Being everywhere means it is eternal.
Being eternal, means everything returns to it.
Tao is great. Heaven is great. Earth is great. Humanity is great.
Within the universe, these are the four great things.
Humanity follows the Earth. Earth follows Heaven.
Heaven follows the Tao. The Tao follows only itself.

Herewith, the Great ones are regarded as descending, from abstract to concrete, taking their power into consideration. A leader deserves to be called *great* not just by her formal position, but as a mediator between the three Great mentioned above. Consider the extraordinary achievements of Hannibal successfully invading the Roman Empire but overall losing the *Second Punic War*—mainly with a lack of a sufficient management structures to assure maintenance of the conquered territories. We better know that only by proper management, one can secure consistent earnings under changing conditions.

With "*I Ching*" introduced between the 10th and 4th centuries BCE, the ancient China took a close look at change effects and ways of managing uncertainty in contest. Remarkably, *Lǎozǐ* then pointed out with "*Tao Te Ching*" to the fundamental principles at meaningful work in all ever-changing shaping. Each technological or economical renovation leads to changes in companies. Change is inevitable in any dynamic environment, and only *open systems*[2] can adapt according to the context—rigid rules have higher chances of failures. When conditions in the external environment don't match assumptions, operations should be able to realign multiple internal processes, ensuring changes get communicated across the organization.

Taoist doctrines often provide reciprocal insights into human interactions, such as knowledge comes from education and learning comes from knowledge. Let's consider their aspects by reviewing
- flexibility in diversity (unified *TAO* and *TE*)

---

[2] See https://en.wikipedia.org/wiki/Open_system_(systems_theory).

- disruptive purpose-driven leadership (*wújí* topics)
- persistent engagement with consistency (*wúwéi* theme)
- flexibility in a natural state (*zìrán* aspects)
- Cyclic Innovation for improvement (fueled by *qi*)
- operational excellence (influenced by *jīng*)
- balanced factors (*shén* perspectives)
- harmony across societies (universal *héxié* values).

TAO and *TE* as Unity in Diversity

We shall aim at overcoming deficiencies in the contemporary society. The tide of change in outward diversification can evolve to inner unity by the means of shared objectives. Leveraging diversity and inclusion at workplace opens chances for comprehensive ways in the adaptation of the multitude of possible options. Appropriate programs of inclusive work setting deploy diversity with a focus on the overall well-being. In

---

We do not easily grasp the point that the void is creative, and that being comes from nonbeing as sound from silence and light from space.

Alan Watts in "Tao: The Watercourse Way".

this section, we want to review the overarching aspects and get a closer look at the essential principles and factors underlying for the experience of best-possible performance toward the desired outcome.

The advantages of the Taoist way of leadership are in the self-realization of employees and in the synergy effects for the organizational flourishing, as outlined below. There are numerous desirable futures in front of us, however, only some of them have potential for achievements of expected business results. The evaluation criteria are important for identification and engagement of expertise to turn encouraging initiatives into a fruitful chronicle. Doing this, it can matter to distinguish the power to know (*TAO*) from ability to execute (*TE*), destiny (*TAO*) from probability (*TE*), intrinsic order (*TAO*) from the continuous process (*TE*), and furthermore.

Absolute structures can support holistic models, whereas specialized areas mostly cover part of the overall supply chain. Such perception might be excelled but not equaled, as stated in the verse 51 of TTC, which points to a challenging act between pursuing autocracy and acknowledging heterogeneity.

> *Tao gives them life. Virtue nurses them,*
> *Matter shapes them, Environment perfects them.*
> *Therefore, all things without exception*
> *worship Tao and do homage to Virtue.*
> *They have not been commanded to workshop Tao and do homage to*
> *Virtue, but they always do so spontaneously.*
> *It is Tao that gives them life, it is Virtue that nurses them, grows them,*
> *fosters them, nourishes them, and covers them under her wings.*
> *To give life but to claim nothing,*
> *To do your work but set no store by it,*
> *To be a leader, not a butcher, this is called hidden Virtue.*

Complex corporations are characterized by connections between different business areas with mutually stabilizing strengths and weaknesses. In all circumstances, there are certain fundamentals (*TAO*) to adhere to, and contextual dynamics that are influencing course of actions (*TE* as virtue). We are going to cover these elements at greater details below. The chances are high to detect reasonable yearning wishes within the set environment with consultative mindset.

The business case for *diversity* is taking place in several appearances: in perspectives and ideas, in workforce providing different backgrounds, but also across our efforts and offerings. Diversity of thought can uncover capabilities through the potential they possess. There are always several ways to proceed when locating barriers. Leaders address complex obstacles in innovative ways so that embraced variety can lead to optimized advanced positioning over rivals. To unlearn our mindset and behavior solely based on experience, we need encounters with some representatives from other cultures or geographies. *Workforce diversity* can better address variety of the external business environments. As a successful manager, one surely wants to uncover various strengths and abilities among your committed and loyal staff. The differences can be about gender and age, cultural matters, educational levels, functional skills, and experience within and outside the corporation. Gender equality could counterbalance biases, which predominate in a patriarchal organization. There seems to be a natural tendency to resist strong dominance or monopoly. We take pleasure in participating in a fair competition.

Established on the unity in diversity, inclusive decision-making appreciates collaboration, sharing, and trust. As it happens, mutual trust in collaboration is the lifeblood to long-term success. It can only arise from actions that are based on shared values. Expressing guiding principles with straight and practical communication skills could reinforce support from followers. Kouzes and Posner clearly state in their "Practice 1" that leaders "*must understand and appreciate the values of their constituents and find a way to affirm shared values.*" (Kouzes and Posner 2012).

Leaders can be flexible and don't stick to a fixed position. Transformational leaders stimulate others to achieve extraordinary outcomes, knowing that they exert influence within their networks and beyond. They are leading by attentively following ideas of others and energizing with personal engagement. With a shared vision and focus on agreed business objectives, it can bring desired position in the marketplace.

> When several attempts to establish a proven solution at the National Bank in a developing country remained fruitless, the managing director

> had to *"put up the sleeves"* and assume personal responsibility for implementation efforts by mobilizing international key subject-matter experts. It surely helped that he could employ better levers to secure expected results. Establishing a formal steering committee with participants from the corporate levels on both sides has ensured good governance and direction, so that succeeding on the resolution of all issues at this strategic account any further issues could be prevented. As the result of established trust, the vendor could find open doors at many commercial banks. The reached outcome of such an engagement can become a contribution to an improved reputation within that industry beyond regional boundaries.

There is no one right way to manage business, as different situations require flexible advances. Providing irrefutable vision and direction is a rare ability of gifted executives. Unfading visions are built on impressions of possible future scenarios. They picture collective desire for a shared target that could be reached by their common efforts.

Safeguarding sustainable results often depend on consensus of shared goals. Even if acting as a samurai in a battle, there is necessity to bring along essential resources. For the assessment of their quality, one needs to collect qualified input from experts. Managerial savvy aiming at overcoming challenges depends on fair accredit of their contributions for the sound proposal on execution.

> To win a strategic deal in a new country under constraint of local resources, it is prudent to share a list of requirements with qualification criteria to the respective product managers as well as services team. By comparing their responses, it gets feasible to evaluate company strengths and challenging positions. Taking into considerations prospect's expectations, your offering shall propose a meaningful framework which structures strengths and weaknesses and outlines necessary services towards reaching the desired state.

A true leader understands value from demanding undemanding. She is humble, *down-to-earth*, without any vanity or hindrance, and able to instinctively set right course derived from past achievements. Where does such *inspiration* come from? Any leader is expected to pursue meaningful goals and objectives and be able to articulate sound strategies for expected growth, and the effects of which will possibly materialize, as has been outlined in the verse 5 of TTC

> *The Tao doesn't take sides; it gives birth to both good and evil.*
> *The Master doesn't take sides; she welcomes both saints and sinners.*
> *The Tao is like a bellows: it is empty yet infinitely capable.*
> *The more you use it, the more it produces;*
> *the more you talk of it, the less you understand.*
> *Hold on to the centre.*

The development of enterprises can be evaluated objectively only by using key performance indicators. We are all accountable to the same fundamental laws, natural and socially. With an understanding of the undifferentiated principles (*TAO*), you will be able to evaluate their influences (*TE*) and detect trends that are worth to be capitalized from the opportunities at hand. The aim is for a fruitful integration, yet with no intention to deal against personal ambitions.

Whenever locating a safe route forward is becoming a challenge, valid leadership rests on the ability to consider major influences. When securing affairs, it's worth to consider the subtle force as it has been outlined in the verse 15 of TTC

> *Who can make the still gradually come to life through activity?*
> *He who embraces this Tao does not want to fill himself to overflowing.*
> *It is precisely because there is no overflowing that he is beyond wearing out and renewal.*

Certain occurrences we cannot fully comprehend could also happen arbitrarily by adjustment with related parts of relevant components. The reliance arises from the own commitment to deliver on promises. Painstaking emergence of faith shows willingness into consistent relationship that ultimately pays off for all parties involved. *Taoist leaders* are known to be benevolent, modest, flexible, transparent, as well as gentle but persistent.

It is unavoidable to have an updated and accurate understanding of the business of your strategic customers from a solution, business, political, and competitive points of view. They appreciate providers that not only supply products but also ideas on improved development. The ability to openly debate underlying assumptions with the readiness to make trade-offs in commonly agreed efforts for execution can be clearly considered as a strength. Competitive advantage keeps one afloat on the troubled sea, as stated in the verse 81 of TTC

> *True words are not beautiful, beautiful words are not true.*
> *The good are not argumentative, the argumentative are not good.*
> *Knowers do not generalize; generalists do not know.*

As expressed in this verse, true flexibility lies in the encouraged adaption to changes, with the ability to avoid traps by gaining depth of insight to the breadth of execution options.

One does not want the own mind to be scattered on everything that is happening around. The ability to persist in the long term is expressed by flexible behavior within changing conditions. Success of any organization largely dependent on its management abilities. Practiced attentiveness expounds what is relevant and how it concerns your current position. Based on their research, Kouzes and Posner have notified that "*the leadership challenge never goes away.*" While courageous leaders can anticipate key trends and consider leaps to distant possibilities, the choices of managers are always oriented toward continuous improvements of the initiated strategic developments.

People can react differently to challenges. With ability for analytical processing, *emotional intelligence* highly matters for business leaders and successful managers.[1] The foundational tenet of emotional intelligence lies in a balanced awareness of self and understanding of others within a coexistent context. It can resonate with high standards of integrity and conflict resolution skills in culturally diverse settings.

> At IBM Laboratories in Germany, it has been prohibited to talk about any business-related tasks in the breaks. Management did not expect employees to maintain the confidentiality of sensitive business information properly. Contrary, at the provider of enterprise software, the "*coffee corner*" culture supports an open exchange of ideas and arguments about any business topic. Every employee gets encouraged to cultivate meeting

---

[1] www.oxford-review.com/blog-how-managers-develop-emotional-intelligence/.

> facilities for exchange. Frequent invitations for topical face-to-face discussions with senior executives open further ways of an update on different positions by the means of a casual conversation with representatives from different lines of business.

For resounding success, it is not enough to make minor adjustments to existing processes. One must be bold in fundamentally changing outdated business models using any available opportunities due to competitiveness at the highest level. Applied *efficiency* is a measurable concept. It depends on flexibility in actions and acceptance within the organization. With all possible intents and purposes, in a truly successful corporation each of the skills is required, provided we make efforts to recognize their distinct qualities. Any duties of executives and line managers are arranged to secure company's performance. Assumed are basic understanding of the accounting principles incl. *accrual method*, business performance with depreciation and amortization, operating growth and net profitability, a new type of linking of internal and external accounting, or the evaluation of customer behavior for regional pricing, etc., can matter to own job duties.

An expansion strategy is a natural move following the saturation of capacity in traditional markets. Open-minded leaders encourage global move with awareness of the diversity among different cultures and markets. It is important to keep an open mindset to whatever emerges. Only when a leader does not enforce the own ambitions can she truly guide others rather than provoke their resistance. Vital energy can freely flow with the ease of limiting restrictions and disturbing conflicts. A relaxed atmosphere helps to strengthen abilities, as expressed in the inception to the verse 55 of TTC

> *Whoever is planted in the Tao will not be rooted up.*
> *Whoever embraces the Tao will not slip away.*

Inner strengths are safeguarding integrity of experienced managers. They will not try to offend all the kinds of emanate entities. Integrity is seen as a basis for credibility. Without a thorough foundation, a rapid upsurge could quickly diminish, while reasoned reflection of achievements with actionable feedback loops enables perspectives for further personal development.

Getting involved within development of emerging markets, one will have to deal with yet unknown regional competition. A greater awareness of their traditions in conducting business and the primary roles of target accounts can be reached only gradually. Companies there prefer contractual terms geared toward win–win relationships. In addition to tangible benefits, intangible improvements can also play an important role here. Clear understanding of assumptions on given conditions and distributed targets from a multiplicity of angles is a fuel in the engine for desired outcome with increased business at a lower cost of account maintenance. With the desire to lead, one needs the ability to anticipate effects of changes. Ways of skillful exchange of information have been well expressed in the verse 27 of TTC

> *Good works are trackless, good words are flawless,*
> *good planning isn't calculating.*
> *What is well closed has no bolt locking it but cannot be opened.*
> *What is well bound has no rope confining it but cannot be untied. ...*

These illustrations exhibit Taoist view to leadership excellence, with comprehending value from guidance and facilitation for efficiency in practical tasks from essential refinement. In-depth experience acquired from awareness of process interdependencies surpasses repeated application of tasks. It's surely better to enable and facilitate new processes, rather than intruding on ongoing operations.

In today's highly competitive business environment, any executive must possess effective leadership skills. They must link accounting principles with strategic planning and efficient operating methods and cater financial means with efficiency toward positive capital turnover. On top, controlling is contributing analytical capabilities to financial controls. Success Across came from their planning session with the tip "*Have your controller on board who can support the leadership team in assigning the correct value for each goal. Equally important, define the bonus factor. Each goal is linked to a defined bonus.*" Sound planning and astute decision-making are among the most influential managerial characteristics to secure success in uncertain times, supported by finance experts with their high levels of creativity and innovation.

> Under the consideration to assume a regional manager position, my company has suggested proper acquirement of financial acumen. Along the creation of the business development plan, all financial key points have been constantly reviewed by assigned controller and approved by higher manager. At the beginning, an active support from controlling experts dealt as risk mitigation. Within a course of financial year, the aim of gaining expected security in plan execution could be achieved. Ability for adaptive management has paid off. After another year, my business plans would pass reviews without any critical remarks. It showed up, that a supervised method to attain practical experience can well lead to expected results from "*learning by doing*". Hence, initially considered attendance at economic courses to obtain MBA degree could be kept off.

There is no one right way to lead. As we can see, fundamental principles (*TAO*) prevail in behavior, and certain techniques (*TE*) assert under given circumstances. We surely need flexibility in the adaptation of different approaches, depending on the desired outcome. To cope with an ongoing change, a nimble enterprise shall be thoroughly adapting to target markets by sharing group-level experience through institutionalized collaboration.

Genuine leaders with Taoist mindset are considering alternating nature of cyclic profits with ongoing costs by virtue of their dual interdependencies. They avoid bedlams from over-utilization of available resources to reach short-term gains and are better off to stretch the quarterly targets to the benefit of large deals and long-term relationships. As an effective leader, one shall be able to secure position of the corporation acting as an agile organization aiming at efficiency—as stressed in the verse 38 of TTC

> *The Master doesn't try to be powerful; thus he is truly powerful.*
> *The ordinary man keeps reaching for power;*
> *thus he never has enough.*
> *The Master does nothing, yet he leaves nothing undone.*
> *The ordinary man is always doing things,*
> *yet many more are left to be done.*

> *The kind man does something, yet something remains undone.*
> *The just man does something, and leaves many things to be done.*
> *The moral man does something, and when no one responds*
> *he rolls up his sleeves and uses force.*
> *When the Tao is lost, there is goodness.*
> *When goodness is lost, there is morality.*
> *When morality is lost, there is ritual.*
> *Ritual is the husk of true faith, the beginning of chaos.*
> *Therefore the Master concerns himself*
> *with the depths and not the surface,*
> *with the fruit and not the flower.*
> *He has no will of his own.*
> *He dwells in reality, and lets all illusions go.*

Influential leaders with ability to articulate their strong opinions succeed without manipulation. Starting from their understanding of underlying business forces of change, they avoid dispensable activities and employ guiding principles by focusing on the sense of clarity in communication. Think of Sakichi Toyoda, considered as father of the Japanese industrial revolution by initiating methodologies to solve problems, improve quality, and reduce costs, gradually leading to *autonomation* in the processes of the lean manufacturing.

All these topics highlight necessity of proper virtues in dealings. Some also try to reach through to the underlying principles within business practices. The triggering question is: how to gain a good business from a poor one? The irregularity in the business world can be seen by the means of the VUCA[2] attributes. Flourishing leaders are on demand when tackling globalization challenges of

- volatility of unpredictable changes with insight and foresight
- uncertainty of critical events with perception and sense
- complexity of cause and effects with comprehensive focus
- ambiguity at paradoxical events with flexible agility.

---

[2] https://en.wikipedia.org/wiki/Volatility,_uncertainty,_complexity_and_ambiguity.

Some business units could struggle to address urgent needs from large deals within emerging markets. Their ability to meet agreed commitments while adapting to changes can be at stake. In addition to higher number of required resources come high-level expectations from the demanding customers on the path for quick catching up in their respective business areas. At this stage, it is pivotal to handpick seasoned experts and proficient project managers for a systematic provision of resources with contributions for expected growth.

> Corporate learning goes hand in hand with knowledge dissemination. Over the course of many years, Deloitte is endowed with depths and breadth of expertise from an established international network in mill and mining. It gained numerous insights from projects in mature and developing countries. After 1990 it's mining & metals business unit leader has been relocated to a subsidiary acting in charge of the Commonwealth of Independent States (CIS). His established reputation in dealing with customers kept local partner companies at guard. As projects size grew, he has ensured that recruiting agencies were engaged to continuously screen the labor market for any consultants with required skills. When needed, he could check out short-listed candidates and get them deployed rather quickly. What a great role model for talent acquisition strategy to be considered.

We should shy away from selective perception in the era of rapid change. Readiness for sustained actions increases with awareness of the factors that are driving change. Autonomy in decision-making by responsible management can be achieved through aligned KPIs.

Taoist approach implies toleration of uncertainty. Proven strategies must be able to stand up to ever shorter market cycles with alternative design options. Most critical processes can be often addressed with methodical structuring or simplification. It is often said that *"just enough is best."* A SWOT analysis can be used periodically to review the current situation, yet not beyond assessment purposes.[3] For this purpose, the essential cornerstones are to be checked and updated.

---

[3] See https://www.chriscorrigan.com/parkinglot/the-taoist-farmer-and-swot-analysis/.

The post-globalization era requires consideration of anticipated global scenarios to protect enterprise position during turbulent times. Changes toward simplified procedures can sometimes require considerable effort. With the necessity of continuous adoption, it is key to determine the essential conditions for achieving the overall goals.

A dynamic VUCA world cannot be simply controlled with a set of sophisticated rules. At best, we can recognize understandable premises and pursue strategic flexibility. Yet, ambitious leaders possess ability in addressing current challenges with a V as vision of benefits from decentralization, U as understanding of advantageous development options, C as expected clarity resulting from an effective GOSPA approach, and A as agility from delegation.

Today's increasingly fragile staff members are expecting leadership authenticity and management transparency. They look forward to clarity in designated priorities and consistency in the execution as essential factors for stability of goal-oriented performance.

You can counteract volatility with coordinated decentralization providing benefits of a secured expansion with smooth communication, motivated management from on-site experience, and ongoing learning efforts. For regional development, decentralization is a tried and tested means of dealing with complexity. Effective leadership is based on the design and control of operational processes. Based on this, the management takes over the organization of structures and the design of processes. It is worth checking again and again the overriding sense of the desired development and the subordinate effectiveness of the activities carried out.

Cohesion requires a meaningful vision and viable strategies to its fulfillment. Only a coherent unit in agreement of statements and behavior can create a basis for good cooperation. Solidarity arises from a common perspective on successful development.

Established trust can be validated through an exchange of favored opinions and proven evaluations. In doing so, deviations in the intentions for further development could be better aligned.

The challenges of disruptions are enormous: the established works less and less, the innovations not quite yet. Agile methodology combines creative experimentation with the review of interim results as a vital opportunity for corrections. In autonomy, the increasing complexity can be conquered with a sense of further development based on intrinsic motivation toward the creation of better conditions.

Reduced levels of predictability call for strategic leadership efforts with prerequisites of flexibility and adaptation. A sound business approach aims at securing sufficient reserves that would allow getting over difficult situations. Upon severe change in conditions, superior process-oriented management shall be able to adjust plans and activities in response—without compromising the far-reaching goals and objectives.

Diverse opposites can constitute through fields of tension. To prevail, an integrative management across various dimensions is required. Inasmuch as one can deliver toward reaching the market-level growth targets, there will be no disturbance to the course of proposed efforts. While opposites exist at the same time, to be more agile and efficient the verse 41 of TTC highlights grasp of non-excluding distinctions.

So there are constructive sayings on this:
the Way of illumination seems dark,
the Way of advancement seems retiring,
the Way of equality seems to categorize,
higher virtue seems empty, great purity seems ignominious,
broad virtue seems insufficient, constructive virtue seems careless.
Simple honesty seems changeable,
great range has no boundaries, great vessels are finished late;
the great sound has a rarefied tone, the great image has no form,
the Way hides its namelessness.
Only the Way can enhance and perfect.

In classical Taoism, any unintentional actions with direct reference to given circumstances are favored. Dealing with ambiguity within a fast-growing, innovative organization requires certain skills of seasoned executives. Only reduced tension can enable creative effects from allegiance to the essential nature of business. Be rest assured that the principles of *TAO* are timeless to guide you safely with the right virtue of *TE*. At length, it's all about awareness and managed adjustment of the key principles to the changing circumstances.

Transformational leadership often takes ownership of results to a construction of an alternative reality—first with the ideation of believers, then from the execution of the followers. The followers deserve to be convinced to higher levels of performance. Any further efforts get justified only if the integrated community receives what they need. Perceived ambiguity in a leader with entrepreneurial capabilities is just fine. At the very least, collaborative goals and shared objectives combined into sound strategies must resonate with group plans and individual actions, as implied in the verse 12 of TTC

> ***Too many colours*** *let you find: they* ***make*** *the* ***human eye go blind****,*
> *are there* ***too many tones*** *to hear: they* ***deafen*** *our* ***human ear****,*
> ***too many flavours*** *soon will* ***waste away*** *the* ***human mouth*** *and* ***taste****.*
> *All* ***battue hunting, horses race****:*
> ***make craze*** *the* ***human heart*** *apace;*
> *all* ***goods*** *too* ***hard*** *to* ***be obtained****,*
> *they* ***cause man's growth*** *to be* ***restrained****.*
> *So* ***wise men care for needs****,* ***not greed****;*
> ***rejecting this****,* ***choose that****, indeed.*

This is a lyrical expression of exaggerations beyond characteristic needs, which could result in sensory overload, exorbitance in expression, and fallacy in taste. Impassioned racing and fervency are confusing, while chasing after rare goods will inhibit maturation and be in the way of viable development. The conclusion is called in the adaptation of John Heider "*When group members have time to reflect, they can see more clearly what is essential in themselves and others.*" (Heider, 2015, p. 12).

Career encounters with mixed cultural contrasts across different business contexts can nurture negotiation and persuasion skills. Surely, there can be resistance to rapid change programs. For a change process, it is appropriate to take sufficient time for alignment with every stakeholder. The inclusive leadership[4] can emerge within respectful teams with shared commitment, leading to effective collaboration from appealing aspirations.

Diversity has a fair potential to become a catalyst for change from a combination of gender, cultural background, and skills in different fields. With a balanced mix of these factors, one can pay off occurring challenges from different perceptions, attitudes, and contributions.

---

[4] See an overview on https://hbr.org/2020/03/the-key-to-inclusive-leadership.

Some members may be driven by accomplishment of their career rather than money. Others might fear an impact on their bonuses. Substantial experience with different cultures is an advantageous asset when getting in charge of engagements in emerging markets. Some paradoxes of the simple substance behind initial appearance get considered in the verse 45 of TTC

> *The greatest accomplishments seem imperfect,*
> *yet their usefulness is not diminished.*
> *The greatest fullness seems empty, yet it will be inexhaustible.*
> *The greatest straightness seems crooked.*
> *The most valued skill seems like clumsiness.*
> *The greatest speech seems full of stammers.*
> *Movement overcomes the cold, and stillness overcomes the heat.*
> *That which is pure and still is the universal ideal.*

Great leaders could remain unperceived, as they avoid interventions knowing established organizational commitments. When shared, key insights can sound naive or unsophisticated. Common sense is fine, provided it does not compromise essential values of leadership providing the moderation of decision-making processes.

Leaders want to overcome the scarcity mindset by leading from a chance of possibility. They are not afraid of the dynamics of self-organizing teams, neither by the passing opinions of communities. Successful leaders estimate the long-term economic nature of a business development, reflecting on their recommendations beyond the fluctuations of quarterly and yearly figures. Understanding the market dynamics, they stay strong in resistance to sudden changes of short-term prospects from interference with competition. Simply relying on scalable efficiency is not an option. They are not afraid to question known prospects and take reasonable risks on the new path.

> Steve Jobs (1955–2011) has demonstrated value from intuition. In particular, his employment with calligraphy led to an interplay of aesthetics and function represented by all Apple Inc. products. With its quality-as-excellence drive, absorptive capacity and durability in offerings, the company has clearly secured competitive advantage. The consumers surely

> appreciate this by high brand loyalty. Tim Cook as current CEO has remarkably stated that the multinational company has a continuous focus on people, strategy, and execution.

A role model leader possesses certain qualities including respect for others, commitment to articulated goals and objectives, and strong ability for collaboration. Joint planning for several market segments could be truly challenging when missing considerations of regional differences and key players there. Market conditions always shift. An expansion into an *emerging market* can be considered as a significant factor for company growth. An extraordinary growth potential in the *developing countries* could partly divert from the core business in matured economies. When expanding into new territories, one needs to assess potential risks and look at partnership with regional players. An effective way could be asking an experienced and trusted fellow to become a sparring partner for each-other thinking.

> For the win at the leading Romanian mobile network operator, we were given the challenge of appropriately staffing an international team for this state-of-the-art project. The result was the selection of a project manager from Canada, subject-matter experts from France, an implementation team from Germany and support teams from India. In combination with the local implementation partners, such a commitment required a thorough introductory phase. With the intention of forming a cohesive team, the senior project manager organized several get-to-know events. There was a joint effort in the creation of a common glossary with the definition of the relevant business terms (by the customer) and associated technological features (by the supplier)—his tool was considered for the foundation of the implementation blueprint. During the execution of the project, a set of system and user documentation has been handed over to the local teams for completion and ownership. Ultimately, this has ensured joint responsibility for the results.

To remain relevant, you will need to maintain further relationships. When niche markets are conquered, they must be protected against upcoming competition. When having scarce resources at hand, one will consider opportunities with the high quality and adjust the own attention to principles and their appearances.

Leadership builds on successful influence. It pays to be accessible and reliable. Critical incidents can happen at any time. It's important to nourish the sense of purpose in every critical venture. With the understanding of a unity in the existing matters, one can orchestrate viable assessment of actions being able to intervene upon compelling events. Proper cognizance of the practices that are critical to quality assurance can ensure changes in the environment as well as key factors that impact stakeholders and group dynamics to form a strategy for desired outcome. A sustainable relationship of trust should be established with every relevant business contact. Only if your peers know which goals are in the foreground can you contribute to their realization. Only by securing trusting relationships with fellows and peers, one can effectively influence interpersonal dynamics so that combined efforts will resonate with cogent objectives. *Taoist leaders* follow fundamental principles while adapting to change. It is sensible to expect the best possible outcome while preparing for possible adversities with feats on the progressing path.

Wújí Within the Company Values

"If you define the problem correctly, you almost have the solution". Steve Jobs

The primary purpose of this section is a review of certain guiding principles relevant for successful corporations. A new development should only be initiated from the knowledge of the real scope and the best-possible weighing of options for action. The exemplary social behavior can strengthen the positive perception of an enterprise. On the following pages, our focus is on the purpose-driven leadership for sustainable business. Common objectives including an indication of the *Corporate Social*

Responsibility (CSR) concept can be treated as a foundation of shared aspirations within the society. Since 2006, the concept of CSR was included in Chinese Corporate Law, to then become mandatory for leading progressing corporations.[1] A Chinese CSR business contingency model tries to address man–nature harmony as an overall balance in connection of internal positions and external perspectives—from lasting loyalty to an increase in the workforce performance.

Many companies are now on a sustainability journey. With the aim to shape a better future, they take on expanded social responsibilities. Most CSR initiatives are oriented on acceptance within broader society, while sustainability relates on adoption of systemic perspectives. With an emphasis on self-sustaining management, strong motivation of surrounding staff aligned to the clear CSR objectives can secure viable outcome on top of considerable values for society. Let's see how the verse 7 of TTC is shading light to long-lasting matters.

> **Eternal Heaven, Earth** *so* **stable. Thus,** *to be* **constant both** *are* **able,** *not for their own they* **do persist, hence,** *they* **can constantly exist.**

An effective leader should be able to maintain a low profile, while attaining results through others. As stated by John Heider "*By being selfless, the leader enhances self*" (Heider, 2015, p. 7). Based on this insight, one can better chart the course for advancement by reviewing, understanding, and applying Taoist principles to yield the bottom line of non-forcing values in coordination of individuals contributing to achievements along the corporate goals and objectives.

So far, we have covered some aspects of holistic management. The terms "*company*" or "*organization*" are used to describe a business entity in the private sector, that is aiming at growth in developing countries, incl. Central and Southeast Asia. A major focus of this section is about affiliation with the company culture under constraints of ongoing transformation efforts. Everyone can benefit from changes in the corporate diversification with the appreciation of *wújí*.

The business agility is paramount to transcend capabilities under changing circumstances. Notable motivation is required when getting

---

[1] See case studies on www.coresponsibility.com/csr-china-follower-leader.

outside comfort zone of achievements toward reaching higher heights. In facilitating social responsibility, leader's effectiveness depends on conviction in own beliefs arising from the inner confidence on how things should be accomplished toward mutual success. Always checking on "What's going on?" will keep the own situational sensing capability up to date. Try to imagine Columbus sailing in the turbulent seas of uncertainty and missing motivation of his crew when the new continent was still behind the horizon. Despite resistance, he was determined and persistent, moving beyond failures.

Managers are asked to review current positions and endorse stock of possible options when considering any substantial change in proposed direction. Insight into the concerns of the employees is beneficial for the business climate. Well-thought-out efforts of consistent adaptation could lead to sensible alternatives or fruitful reflections. Otherwise, new initiatives would either stall or even fail to achieve intended results. Among the key attributes of *servant leadership* are authenticity, interpersonal acceptance that encourages reflective backtalk, and stewardship while empowering and developing others. Such characteristics are based on Taoism and can result in significant success. Trust emerges from their care on building and sustaining a reputation for reliability in maintaining interconnections.

> It has been a real pleasure in dealing with an open-minded CIO at a growing financial institution. His desire was flexible reconfiguration of business models to keep pace with disruption. Understanding of the requirements was key. With the contribution of data analysis and modelling capabilities, he could then drive adaptation of industry-specific representation of business lines to the systematic enterprise-wide integration. By uncovering underlying interdependencies across all departments, the implementation of these measures was key for systematic improvements from collaboration across all units to predictable outcomes. The value-add for the board-level stakeholders was provision of sophisticated metrics that include customer loyalty and partner views for improved investor relationship.

It's often best to clarify what obstacles stand at the intersection of possible alternatives for a company culture with an open team spirit.

Prior to a challenging undertaking, there are often perceived views of the desired end state. The originator of cybernetics, Norbert Wiener (1894–1964) has pointed out the subtle difference of the leadership position in "*knowing what*" to "*knowing how*". Management prefers to act within their *circle of competence,* trying to prevent questionable expenses including associated bureaucratic costs.

Corporate policies and organizational rules aim at regulation of employee behaviors. Clearly defined company-wide values can affect organizational attitudes, which then lead devoid of coercion to widely accepted exploits. By contrast, individual motivational orientation can contribute to a variety of diverse approaches—especially when supported by managerial attributions with a clear sense of purpose from the ability to active listening resulting in effective feedback.

Whatever you do at work, it shall be according to the core values of the company you are working for. It's about acting on behalf of the vivid wholeness without putting personal interests in the foreground. Junior employees expect to be motivated by superior knowledge. They measure their achievements from participation in rewarding projects. Such aptitude requires confidence in the competence of coworkers. Consider their traits to judge if it's worth getting engaged. By supporting the abilities of others, any arising potential for a conflict can be avoided. Repeatedly, it's about integrity and alignment across organization, as expressed with metaphors in the verse 35 of TTC

> *When holding the Great Image,*
> *the world goes on and on without harm: peaceful, even, tranquil.*
> *Where there is music and dining, passing travellers stop;*
> *But the issue of the Way is so plain as to be flavourless.*
> *When you look at it, it is invisible;*
> *when you listen to it, it is inaudible;*
> *when you use it, it cannot be exhausted.*

A boost of motivation is required under challenging circumstances. A leading skill without exhausting could be associated with an extraordinary sensitivity to others as ability to "*look behind the scenes*" or *sight-reading*. Being open-minded, one can adapt to new trends and ways of collaboration.

Purpose-driven leadership aligns any inevitable business decisions with essential principles. With the need to change established business, leaders of such caliber don't shy away from unorthodox ideas.[2] By constantly monitoring the dynamics of business life, they are always ready to apply adjustments to processing—without getting lost in negligible particularities. For any aberrant proposals, they rely on inner judgment and consider alternative views and contributions.

No one can any longer compromise on sustainability. Related business models, concepts, and perspectives are on the raise. Ecological sensitivity within corporations is twofold: it gets partly regulated by corporate procedures (i.e., controlled access to printers) while alongside also prompting pro-environmental consciousness of employees.

> The leader in business applications defines success more broadly than just financial performance by following the motto *"Helping the World run better and improving peoples lives"*. Its move into *sustainability* aiming at *"integrating economic, environmental and social performance to drive better decision-making"* grew to become another key initiative. The company is getting expressive revenue from its multi-facet offerings and solutions with respect to the UN *Sustainable Development Goals* following a principles-based approach. It pays off in many facets, from sustainability measures within a yearly report to new innovative products and services.

Approved total goals should be coherent and appropriate to the real circumstances. The successful managers grasp shared values to ensure that cooperative behavior contributes to a productive outcome. Their persistence in attaining organizational goals pays off with the valuable contributions to profitable growth. Striking greatness from selfless service is well expressed in the verse 34 of TTC

The great Tao flows everywhere.
All things are born from it, yet it doesn't create them.
It pours itself into its work, yet it makes no claim.
It nourishes infinite worlds, yet it doesn't hold on to them.

---

[2] Outlined in https://jcsr.springeropen.com/articles/10.1186/s40991-019-0041-z.

> *Since it is merged with all things and hidden in their hearts,*
> *it can be called humble.*
> *Since all things vanish into it and it alone endures,*
> *it can be called great.*
> *It isn't aware of its greatness; thus it is truly great.*

Leaders are often seen as a difference-maker. Considerably contributing to an expanding intrinsic value of a company, they add value to everyone in their networks and beyond. Steve Chandler apprises that often among the hardest obstacles is our own inner resistance. It's then surely worth to pause and passionate review possible causes of uncertainty. Rather than being engrossed on any real and potential problems, considerations of possible solutions will contribute to a way out of burdensome concerns. Ability to detect common principles among constituents, best paired with confidence and self-awareness exhibited in ambiguous situations, can encourage others in pursuit of shared objectives. An accomplished leader, by acting impartial without interference, will avoid both to spare her subjects any embarrassment. Troubles will be inevitable if the leader's personality traits suffer from explicit self-references. Her favorable attributes are intellectual approach to the realm and emotional aspect for the comprehensive suitability of astute guidance.

> An early lesson in my career was the constant link of personal beliefs to the overall objectives of the employer organization. Working in the support structure for the customers across European countries at that stage allowed deep level of understanding for their requirements. This background led to a secondment as developer in the global headquarters as ambassador of the European customers. The engagement has led to improvements in the offered products and gained insights became a foundation in the following customer-facing roles.

There are ways to transform any challenge into productive opportunities—if we evolve to holistic views of the entangled world. Great leaders contribute to aspirations of their constituents, providing information on the progress toward the common goals. Making sure to enlist others into a success story is a powerful gear to strengthen common purpose. Sometimes, with assurance that they are riding an enduring trend, managers would lean back. They often prefer to concentrate on the most significant projects to capitalize on.

A structured experience-based learning agility can be provided by skilled *facilitators*.[3] Driven by purpose, it's rewarding to experience a refinement upon having established a collaborative process. Simply put, just be content with your tasks and let the universe do the rest.

> The market leader in enterprise application regularly brings together key account managers with experts from product development, services organizations, and partner companies. Ahead of the industry-centric workshops, structured input gets collected from parties having stake in growth and stability of selected accounts. Criteria for participation is around industry relevance with provision of sound use cases. At kick-off, leaders outline major trends in that industry and showcase key innovations, including partner solutions. A major benefit comes from focused discussions about individual accounts that get initiated by the presentation of the account manager to those who are interested in providing their assistance from different business areas. Upon review of the current situation, known issues get outlined so that new opportunities can be considered. Central peace is a "cross pollination" session towards the best practices exchange and collection of sparkling ideas.

> The duty of the designated facilitator is to have everyone in the meeting room participate in the considerations for improvements, then move it along by keeping track of an action list. He/she stimulates creative thinking by the means of a collaborative review of innovative opportunities. In charge of driving the collaborative opportunity generation sessions, they ensure a desired impact for every contributor. Their leadership skills in motivating participants and streamlining discussions are of critical importance for success of such events. The facilitator bundles synergy by ensuring that newly uncovered opportunities get entered into the CRM system for the follow-up. Overall, the basis for success lies in the effectiveness of the facilitators and follow-up activities with measurable

---
[3] See section on Skills in https://en.wikipedia.org/wiki/Facilitator.

> impact on pipeline management. Higher management certainly expects to see the best choices been effectively implemented.

Taoist leaders can be characterized by their ability for the *lateral thinking*.[4] Its approach at creation of desired impact lies in finding unconventional ways of problem-solving. Important decisions in business are best when done under considerations of shared values. Any qualitative improvement of a familiar "*norm*" can increase the degree of satisfaction and thereby improves the willingness to perform. There are several strategic management models that aim at improvement of an organizational performance.

In particular, "*Management by objectives*" (MbO) has proven to be supporting a self-organizing pattern via objective agreements within companies. Therein, top management expresses syntactical form of internal coordination by the means of *delegation of authority* within explicit regulations and semantic forms within relations to peers and subordinates. Any broader responsibility for results can be expected by assigning subordinates higher latitude for decision-making. Monitoring agreed and interlinked measures contributes to accountability and better discipline. In comparison with Western MbO approach with specific target setting, Eastern management style has much stronger emphasis on "*leading*" by example and "*to foster*" achievements within social responsibility. The verse 26 of TTC outlines compelling aspects of naturalistic turn in administration.

> *Gravity is the root of lightness; calm is the master of excitement.*
> *Thereby do exemplary people travel all day*
> *without leaving their equipment.*
> *Though they have a look of prosperity,*
> *their resting place is transcendent.*
> *What can be done about heads of state*
> *who take the world lightly in their own self-interest?*
> *Lack of gravity loses servants of state;*
> *instability loses heads of state.*

---

[4] See https://en.wikipedia.org/wiki/Lateral_thinking.

These statements show the way to coolness and serenity in avoiding the traps of temptations and by solving difficulties even before they arise. A down-to-earth leader can keep balance and overcome critical situations. Such leaders do not depart from the rules of responsibility, and their powers of reasoning are directed toward purposive adaptation of relevant facts.

Upon insights into effects from introduced changes, the board can readily consider a scale-up option and put a dynamic roll-out planning into action that enables controlled improvements in business practices by limiting negative consequences. Certain pitfalls in the planning can be avoided by considerations of alternative developments. As they occur, scenarios arise to better engage with established content and available resources. Taoism perceives a self-referential acting critically, as outlined in the verse 13 of TTC.

> *Favour and disgrace seem alarming;*
> *high status greatly afflicts your person.*
> *What are favour and disgrace?*
> *Favour is the lower:*
> *get it and you're surprised, lose it and you're startled.*
> *This means favour and disgrace are alarming.*
> *What does high status greatly afflict your person?*
> *The reason we have a lot of trouble is that we have selves.*
> *If we had no selves, what troubles would we have?*
> *Therefore, those who embody nobility to act for the sake of the world*
> *seem to be able to draw the world to them,*
> *While those who embody love to act for the sake of the world*
> *seem to be worthy of the trust of the world.*

Reversion and alternation belong to the viable circulation in fruitful development. The ability to trustful co-operation is key to success or failure of any kind of partnership. Expressions of favor and disgrace are rather unstable and can change into each other, especially for managers in a higher hierarchical position.

Mutual exchange is an unavoidable conclusive feature of business connections. We can share the overall *sense of purpose* by adopting *circular economy* principles of reciprocal relationships. Often, it is demanding to determine effects of long-term economic value from the innovations within changing environment. The understanding of options for improvements under considerations of perceived benefits and anticipated risks contributes to competitive advantage.

It's worth to table expected tangible return and intangible benefits from new exertion. An optimization of targets may come at the expense of value-oriented development. Ability for cyclic evaluation of innovative processes requires flexibility in value-oriented controlling with a focus on performance management. A bench test can serve as framework to stay on track and measure interim results. Latent potential could be maximized, promoting intangible assets to get the most out of available tangible assets.

Managers in turn are expected to ensure contributions to the specified objectives, supervise their team members, and evaluate their performance. There are certain trends that can bring challenges to an effective coordination across vital organizations. A multi-perspective view of a diverse yet aligned team sheds light on how to ask subordinates for an extra mile in their efforts.

In this chapter, we have partly addressed some fundamental aspects of the purpose-driven leadership and management. Let's now look at how reliable behavior could be framed under Taoist principles.

Wúwéi in the Management of Affairs

> *"Doing nothing can sometimes be the most effective form of action".*
> Kevin Kwan in *"Crazy Rich Asians"*

An integrated approach to project and people management becomes essential for corporations to succeed in the twenty-first century. The Taoist concept of "*doing by not doing*" or "*letting things take their own course*" might sound odd at first sight yet is important to contemplate. François Quesnay (1694–1774) made attempt to transform this concept into the *laissez-faire* economic system, which even inspired

Adam Smith (1723–1790) while he established the principles of free-market economics. Alan Watts (1915–1973) believed that *wúwéi* can be best described as a "*non-coercive*" action, while sinologist Jean F. Billeter describes it as a "*state of perfect knowledge of the reality of the situation, perfect efficaciousness and the realization of a perfect economy of energy*". Each decision to either proactive act for a desired impact or restraint to "*let it become*" depends on the dialectical understanding of intentions concerning awareness of a particular state within ongoing affairs. With attention to process, any decisions could have critical organizational impact. This section focuses on *wúwéi* as it stands for non-coercive activities in alignment with the surroundings.

Market research is perceived as an important component of business strategy and a major factor in maintaining competitiveness. There are some subtle elements in the business culture within Greater China worth thorough considerations. They anticipate senior executives to set up strategies and structures, while having line management to execute with minimum interference. Long-term orientation in closing deals and "*saving face*" in resolving issues are among the best known there. Its stewards often show acknowledgment for readiness to adaptation and flexibility in the application of proven methodologies. According to "China Daily", the well-known *wúwéi* approach is quite common across Chinese businesspeople. Based on the school of thought that *TAO* principles are always manifested in *TE* as market-based mechanisms, they expect organization to perform on its own. Initiated actions shall be based on a thorough investigation into specific properties for each considered claim. It has been experienced that inconceivable potential of alternative options can also lie in the state of *non-doing*, rather than swiftly wasting any available resources in business misconduct. Partly, because the political leadership with dictatorial impulses began to divide the world into zones of influence, so that efforts toward self-sufficient economic activity are emerging again.

Proper guidance could be crucial for effective participation in the realization of important undertakings. It is often about the nuances in the interaction of individuals and companies in the framework set by the community. When in a structural transition, it might be better if certain managers refrain from wrongdoing. Warren Buffett's descriptive "*Rule

No. 1: Never lose money" (Buffett & Clark, 2008, p. 3) is deceptively simple yet enormously powerful in application.

> A valid example for *wúwéi* approach is *"the way of Warren Buffet"*. His investment method is based on conceivable principles, while his strategy is taking long-term development trends into considerations. Research published at the University of Oxford characterizes Buffett's investment methodology as falling within *"founder centrism"*, defined by a deference to managers with a founder's mindset, an ethical disposition towards the shareholder collective, and an intense focus on exponential value creation. It may seem that his intuition is formed around basic financial rules, his instincts rely on proven observations, and his decisions depend on compression and reduction analysis. In his business lecture at the University of Florida School of Business back in 1998 he stated *"Wall Street makes its money on activity. You make your money on inactivity"*. In a nutshell, it suggests avoiding excessive activity but concentrate application of right decision at best chosen time and place for sustainable development.

The *wúwéi* principle is about unbiased practice of the authority without disturbing interfering a natural course by unnecessary ventures. Thought leaders don't hesitate in challenging set procedures by adapting them to advanced processes. They know how to act effectively without any expectation of unreachable goals. An effective leader does not set unrealistic goals. She underlines any ability to strengthen peers on the path of the least resistance. Only with objectives adjusted to reasonable outcomes, the expected achievements can be obtained with relatively small but acute accomplishments. The desired outcome happens effortless if one is in accord with the reality. A lesson on yielding passivity from the verse 63 in TTC can be linked to the common knowledge *"Focus on the big picture but start small"*.

> Be **doing**, yet **without ado**, do **business**, *free from bustling*, too,
> the **tasteless** even let **taste great**, find **big** in **little**, much in **few**,
> with **Inner Power** answer hate.

We can view this thoroughgoing invocation as a stimulation of lasting vigor in leadership and management free of conflict and coercion. Deliberate avoidance of preconceived ideas increases chances for contributions from people involved. Curiosity opens up the mind to see things from different angles in stepwise improvements.

Within the Taoist context, leaders are guiding from abstract ideas of the reasonable outcomes supporting transition to the management of reachable tasks. They solve problems more effectively by clearly recognizing the current state in the larger notion. Notably, this verse in particular highlights *attention to detail*.

> ***Plan difficulties, while they're plain,***
> ***do greatness while it's small****, again.*
> *For **all world's difficulty springs** quite **certainly from easy things;***
> *and **all world's great affairs mature from marginal** ones**, to be sure.***

In business, that means review of financial effects as well as interpersonal implications from the implementation of the own proposal.

Taking note of a double attribution of cause and effect, we shall distinguish between decision premises and possibilities of actions.

> ***For easy promise, little trust, much ease—much trouble*** *to adjust.*

Ultimately, the conclusion of this verse is

> ***So, wise men face*** *the **trouble's** call,*
> ***hence, free of problems, after all!***

Everyone shall react timely and reasonably when an encounter arises so that it can lead up into a mutually positive outcome. Any difficult business situations can get resolved through properly managed team efforts.

Contentment with achieved results creates a state for further possibilities. Availability of uncommitted time leaves room for further novel opportunities, while enforced changes are not durable. Taoism favors those who get along well with little interference, as expressed in the verse 80 of TTC

> *A small state has few people.*
> *It has the people keep arms but not use them.*
> *It has them regard death gravely and not go on distant campaigns.*
> *Even if they have vehicles, they have nowhere to drive them.*
> *Even if they have weapons, they have nowhere to use them.*

Wúwéi in the Management of Affairs 57

> *It has the people to go back to simple techniques,*
> *relish their food, like their closes,*
> *be comfortable in their ways and enjoy their work.*
> *Neighbouring state may be so close*
> *they can hear each other's dogs and roasters,*
> *but they make it so that the people have never gone back and forth.*

It's worth to consider that simplicity contributes to freedom. This utopia expresses a domain with simple customs yet at good sense of mutual understanding, that is avoiding excess and is relying on the available capabilities without any distraction.

Obviously, the Taoist believes have codified Chinese views on the corporate behavior. They await benefits from the reflection of *gain* from adherence to natural inaction, even if resulting in *loss* by release of burden from needless interventions. As an illustration, let's review lessons from a story on the "Rise of the Tao" published in 2010 by *The New Your Times Magazine*.

> Zhengzhou owes its existence to the intersection of two railway lines. One of the largest markets there is the five-story "Phoenix City" with over 4 million square feet of showroom. On the roof of this mall is the mansion of Zhu Tieyu. His early career was devoted to money making as enrichment. As he got older, he started thinking more about cultural wisdom and the rules by which people preferred to live there. By following the Taoist principles of patience and appropriateness of actions, the now prosperous businessman gradually became acknowledged *"king of the building materials"*. His "Henan Xinshan Taoist Culture Propagation Company" has meanwhile established many forums to discuss and promote Taoism in China.

Getting into the emerging markets and confronted with unanticipated regulation's flexibility in management should allow for the necessary contingency planning. As risk-takers, leaders can foresee a well-intentioned failure. In challenging situations, they aim at balance in relationships by skillful use of praise and tactful articulation of critical factors to be considered. Managerial duties in clarification of conflicts and facilitation of processes are to some degree expressed in the verse 20 of TTC

> *Stop thinking and end your problems.*
> *What difference between yes and no?*
> *What difference between success and failure?*
> *Must you value what others value, avoid what others avoid?*
> *How ridiculous!*
> *Other people are excited, as though they were at a parade.*
> *I alone don't care, I alone am expressionless,*
> *like an infant before it can smile. ...*

Rather than considerations of what school of thought applies, an application of a sound judgment in practical matters brings better results. Being content with an all-round approach prevents inconvenience and ensures accomplishments and achievements sustainably.

A well-thought-out strategy is about gaining an advantage following beyond present conditions with flexible and efficient matters and affairs practiced across the peers. The best argument in a sales strategy is about the relevance and contribution of own product's respective services to the business of their target customers. How to keep high customer satisfaction levels? Incremental sales shall be according to their contemporary needs that go hand in hand with the capability in the implementation of expected results, as somewhat articulated in the verse 30 of TTC

> *Whoever relies on the Tao in governing men*
> *doesn't try to force issues or defeat enemies by force of arms.*
> *For every force there is a counterforce.*
> *Violence, even well intentioned, always rebounds upon oneself.*
> *The Master does his job and then stops.*
> *He understands that the universe is forever out of control,*
> *and that trying to dominate events*
> *goes against the current of the Tao.*
> *Because he believes in himself, he doesn't try to convince others.*
> *Because he is content with himself, he doesn't need others' approval.*
> *Because he accepts himself, the whole world accepts him.*

It's far better to do "nothing" than worsening a situation through self-infatuation or disturbing activities to the natural course of actions.

Whenever having performed well, good leaders do not need to show off, they do not require vain sense of triumph. Their conviction will spark over anyway.

We can acknowledge that a governance derived from Taoist values has been arguably implemented at *Haier Group Corporation* by its CEO *Zhang Ruimin* due to his mental agility, adopting traditional Chinese management practices to new management concepts.[1] Let's see how the meaning of *wúwéi* principle blended with the Chinese cultural values could influence on development strategies.

> The Haier Group, located in Quigdao, has evolved under the leadership of Zhang Ruimin from producing refrigerators for local market to become an electronics multinational corporation. The foundation of considerable achievements was laid by customer's loyalty due to quality of manufactured products. Innovations were encouraged and rewarded. Major production reengineering was caused by tough competition during marketization. As an assertive leader, the CEO has introduced quality controls for improvements. His role in the management of change was to set up reliable best practices within operations. Major phases in development have been brand building (with application of total quality management program), diversity-in-unity for product offerings, and expansion by trusted dealer networks. Joint ventures contributed to inception of advanced management practices. As far-sighted leader, Zhang Ruimin could always foresee the upcoming transitions in the legislation and make corresponding adjustments to further explore market potential. In line with the legislative support, the Group grew by applying quality into production processes in the turmoil of policy changes. CEO has managed to shift from a function based to market chain-oriented process. Instead of normative control, each department became a strategic business unit with focus on distinct customers. Performance measurement was in place for the core and supporting processes. Improvement of services could accompany creation of innovative products. Guided by liberalization, sound diversification played a major role in the expansion phase—conducted in a series of mergers and acquisitions. Acting as an autocratic leader, the CEO has assumed the role of a change agent. The application of Taoist principles within Chinese culture has taken significant part in the management of the corporation, so that Western practices could be adopted in accordance with the frequent change requirements.

---

[1] www.imanet.org/-/media/bfbff080097e4a9089971cea342177aa.ashx.

> Impartiality was key to ensure agreement with the workforce upon an incentive system built on open criteria. Constant change management has been held up with regular briefings of senior and line management. Following China's accession to WTO, further growth in the US and higher returns to investments abroad came under considerations.

Each successful enterprise needs discipline, dedication, and top-down governance, all leading to skilled execution of a highly cultivated way. Upon remastering enterprise performance management, leadership could be rather considered from a holistic rather than taxonomic perspective. It could be helpful to portray and rate relevant product portfolio by using the *Boston matrix*[2] as an aiding tool for competitiveness and demand estimation. It fits rather well to the balanced Taoist management perspectives.

Customer expectations are growing swiftly. When it comes to change management, large corporations favor a top-down approach. They prefer an innovative solution to be initially implemented in a smaller branch, prior to a decision for its roll-out to other entities in dependence to results. Meanwhile, most leading companies within emerging markets are well connected with their peers from mature countries as a partner in closing gaps by building bridges in pursuing win–win collaboration.

> Winning a World Bank tender for the National Bank of Bulgaria, it was commanded to visit Sofia and establish ties with professional services companies there. Going forward, we could initiate a "Proof-Of-Concept" project with the UniCredit Bulbank. Further on, it led to a meeting with one of the directors at the Statistical Office, who's peers have been already using our software and served as reference. Going forward, we agreed on their participation in a topical event.

For a new beginning, an unbound action is often the best way to go. An emphatic leader can motivate others in multiplication of efforts while avoiding ambitions that can cause separation. The *wúwéi* approach

---

[2] https://www.tutor2u.net/business/reference/boston-matrix-and-product-portfolios.

implies avoidance of unnecessary actions toward domination but rather relies on genuine confidence as source for effective actions, as outlined in the verse 3 of TTC

> *If you overly esteem talented individuals,*
> *people will become overly competitive.*
> *If you overvalue possessions, people will begin to steal.*
> *Do not display your treasures or people will become envious.*
> *The Master leads by emptying people's minds;*
> *filling their bellies, weakening their ambitions,*
> *and making them become strong.*
> *Preferring simplicity and freedom from desires,*
> *avoiding the pitfalls of knowledge and wrong action.*
> *For those who practice not-doing, everything will fall into place.*

Talents with integrity and knowledge are seen as the lifeblood of a company. Only motivated employees are powering your business. How certain can results be expected? Management would improve the performance of a team by strengthening common objectives rather than emphasizing exceptional contributions—the later can even become a limiting factor to original talents, that best unfold within open-minded surroundings.

When working with critical clients, often patience bordering on slowness must be exhibited. There is a strong need to match the proposed offering with their reality. Upon thorough investigation, ideally being confirmed by an insider, the proponent must be in position to express benefits from the offering by intelligently combining in-house findings with proven industrial trends. Personal modesty with the professional will to shape things in related areas of business life works best.

> One of my business prospects has been in a rapid expansion mode. My initial offering was on the consolidation of results for improved performance and effective profitability gains. Yet, company board put preference towards creating a broader presence on the market. By reallocation of available funds, they decided to put our project on hold. We discussed advancement options with the buying center and agreed on the ongoing monitoring of the market demands. Upon promotion, my prime contact was ready for the reconciliation of their results. We managed to

> implement the agreed project scope. It paid off to be patient for the right conditions to occur.

Traditional approaches of management schools perform well under known circumstances, but in the context of unknown, flexible novel initiatives are needed. Tolerating unforeseen uncertainty requires a notion of continuous learning and change, even if iterations become time-consuming. Unpredictable chain of activities might as well disrupt the context and influence behavior beyond boundaries of the enterprise to affect partner, supplier, and customer organizations.

Any overemphasis on proven success factors can lead to malfunctions without balancing safeguards. Thought leaders with Taoist mindset understand that in a long run, employee behaviors cannot be coerced. They rather adopt *wúwéi* as an effective way to achieve best results with little efforts from the very beginning, as has been expressed in the stimulating features within the verse 64 of TTC

> *Things are easier to control while things are quiet.*
> *Things are easier to plan far in advance.*
> *Things break easier while they are still brittle.*
> *Things are easier hid while they are still small.*
> *Prevent problems before they arise.*
> *Take action before things get out of hand.*
> *The tallest tree begins as a tiny sprout.*
> *The tallest building starts with one shovel of dirt.*
> *A journey of a thousand miles starts with a single foot step.*
> *If you rush into action, you will fail.*
> *If you hold on too tight, you will loose your grip.*
> *Therefore the Master lets things take their course*
> *and thus never fails.*
> *She doesn't hold on to things and never looses them.*
> *By pursing your goals too relentlessly, you let them slip away.*
> *If you are as concerned about the outcome*
> *as you are about the beginning,*
> *then it is hard to do things wrong.*

Attention to accomplishments, following *precautionary principle* limits potential for causing harm, especially when intense knowledge on the matter is lacking. It acknowledges that while the growth has often brought benefits to the enterprise, this could also contribute to the creation of new threats and risks. *Taoist leaders* remain in a ready state to enhance promising positions with new offerings. They are aware of traits that streamline efforts in exploiting the advantages of every qualified undertaking. Especially, the detection of new beginnings, when slight interventions could have significant effects, can be of particular importance.

A high degree of simplicity needs to be utilized within effective business processes. What matters is an unbiased focus on the completion of current tasks. Reduced complexity with non-interfering in needles affairs factors to higher merits, as outlined in the verse 37 of TTC

> *Tao never makes any ado, and yet it does everything.*
> *If a ruler can cling to it, all things will grow of themselves.*
> *When they have grown and tend to make a stir, it is time to keep them in their place by the aid of the nameless Primal Simplicity, which alone can curb the desires of men.*
> *When the desires of men are curbed, there will be peace,*
> *And the world will settle down of its own accord.*

In a nutshell, Taoism is about dynamic balance in a desired mix of taking and giving.

How can be able leaders guiding in a way that stimulates positive outcome of their followers? Being generous, they have ability and competence to motivate others upon deliberation. It starts with continuous collection of information in the business context that paired with their insights into complex relationships leads to profound non-differentiated knowledge. Next, it is their ability to combine relevant factors into a valid response to uncertain situations. Such an aptitude involves a mix of observational and cognitive skills. Ultimately, when complacency needs challenging, they can tune in with a new direction and business model around distinctive competencies.

Foresighted leaders are continuously looking for learning experience, while meticulous managers concentrate on the execution of routine tasks.

Later can contribute to change by looking for inconsistencies in assumptions on objectives, as well as seeing cause-effect relationships across planning activities. Non-intrusive leaders are superior at making decisions when conditions fit to their foresight. Under higher degree of unpredictability, they prefer to refrain from getting engaged. The risk is that unresolved issues could stack up. It's better to not dwell on a wrong decision and go on with it than to miss fortunate slot for right ones. Warren Buffett has stated with one of his maxims that to earn an adequate rate of return, *"You only have to do a very few things right in your life so long as you don't do too many things wrong."* (Buffett & Clark, 2008, p. 84). Quite often *"Less is more"*, as it has been outlined in the conclusion of the verse 48 in TTC

> *In pursuit of knowledge, every day something is added.*
> *In the practice of the Tao, every day something is dropped.*
> *Less and less do you need to force things,*
> *until finally you arrive at non-action.*
> *When nothing is done, nothing is left undone.*
> *True mastery can be gained*
> *by letting things go their own way.*
> *It can't be gained by interfering.*

The Taoist meaning of learning suggests gaining affective knowledge by affiliation to the flow of natural development. Rather than constantly collecting any further theories and techniques, the unhindered application of already proven methodologies should always be in the foreground.

One might be pleased to comprehend that under the assumption of *"survival of the fittest"* the wúwéi principle means proactive doing by *"thinking outside the box"*. It is surely not sufficient just to initiate a new direction. Successful leaders back up development of suggested initiative tirelessly.

There is an understanding that humble leaders are at their best.[3] This characteristic has been expressed in the verse 61 of TTC as follows

---

[3] Stated in https://oxford-review.com/oxford-review-encyclopaedia-terms/leader-humility-definition-and-explanation/.

When a country obtains great power, it becomes like the sea:
all streams run downward into it.
The more powerful it grows, the greater the need for humility.
Humility means trusting the Tao, thus never needing to be defensive.
A great nation is like a great man:
When he makes a mistake, he realizes it.
Having realized it, he admits it.
Having admitted it, he corrects it.
He considers those who point out his faults
as his most benevolent teachers.
He thinks of his enemy as the shadow that he himself casts.
If a nation is centred in the Tao, if it nourishes its own people
and doesn't meddle in the affairs of others,
it will be a light to all nations in the world.

Dynamic response to evolving circumstances is best under comprehensive consideration of major influencing factors. Great leaders prefer to be receptive and respectful to a stream of relevant ideas. Continuously holding to the prime needs is their ability to support others. They prefer non-pretending provision of service, yielding reciprocal trust and gaining benefits from spontaneous cooperation within the relationship with peers and subordinates.

An effective organization needs clarity in the distribution of roles, with clear responsibilities to assume ownership of assigned tasks—often expressed for stakeholders by the means of a *RACI matrix*.[4] Chances for a triumph depend on the grade of commitment by all those who are affected by initiative, as well as support of executive management. For the good ideas to be realized and not fizzle out, a successful leader ensures that he can establish his followers in important positions to ensure that things run smoothly within innovative value chains. This requires a coordination of decisions, which on the one hand had to be made dynamically concerning local conditions, while taking into consideration the overarching objectives.

Aiming to succeed, one must adapt to the constant changes, while the own advantage lies in the in-depth knowledge of local conditions, which is essential for entrepreneurial success. Viable solutions to challenges at

---

[4] See https://en.wikipedia.org/wiki/Responsibility_assignment_matrix.

stake cannot occur in the concealment of a remote office. Often, only their explicit value independence leads to growth. Therefore, the upper-level position can get extraordinary proxies as instruments of power for execution.

> For the business of a *branch office* the valid *Power of attorney* entitled me to represent the company before all and any local state authorities, institutions, organizations, companies, and individuals. That included explicit rights to
> - negotiate, supervise the implementation, and execute local contracts and other arrangements;
> - employ and discharge employees of the regional office;
> - apply for all and any licenses and permissions for the proper operation, besides applicable registrations and accreditations;
> - open, operate and close necessary bank accounts with the right of the first signature on the banking documents;
> - perform any payments in connection with the representative office;
> - take or participate in any legal actions related to the rightful protection of the interests of the representative office;
> - take all and any other actions and actions deemed necessary or appropriate for the proper operation and maintenance of the representative office.

Let's now see on how to best prevail under continuously changing conditions by illustrations outlined within the following chapter.

Ziràn in the Course of Events

> "The price of success is hard work, dedication to the job at hand, and the determination that whether we win or lose, we have applied the best of ourselves to the task at hand". Vince Lombardi

Taoist approach is certainly emphasizing leadership aspects of management skills in complex relationships within dynamic business world. Success of joint activities is a highly relationship-forming experience. In teams with different skills, each member should be able to consider their own strengths and weaknesses. That creates a need to learn from the experiences of others. A liability arises from reciprocal actions. This is how teamwork develops to achieve more together than would be possible for each member. Recognition leads to respect, while trust comes from understanding. This section outlines a core meaning of insightful leadership in the context of perpetual comprehensive business responsibilities. Those in the state of the natural flow *zirán* are capable of participation in longstanding development, while securing a well-grounded and ordered companionship.

No businessperson can afford to make false claims, although time and again some statements that can harm oneself may be suppressed. How to get ahead of any enforced changes, mostly perceived as disruption? One shall challenge imagination, tolerance, and reputation, fostering an established network to materialize essential ideas. Most leaders define goals and objectives without prescribing detailed plans for their implementation. Besides, they need to be able to evaluate uncertain situations and define a strategy to overcome unprecedented obstacles. Monitoring of results or any deviations in a combination with viable feedback loops are keeping enterprise on the set track within strategic planning.

Even knowing about the fundamental principles (*TAO*) in our being, we often follow uncharted ways (*TE*) as they unfold, depending on circumstances. *Zirán* is another key concept in Taoism that literally means "*of its own, by itself*" with connotation such as "*naturally, freely, certainly*". It could serve as a metaphor for human freedom, as best results can only be achieved with authentic business acumen. Trying to act following *natural flow* could be an effortless attempt. Yet, how to get there? Great leaders always need to be receptive to the ongoing flow of considerations within their areas of influence. By overlooking priorities within compelling events, their preference is on using driving forces rather than applying fragmented moves. A breakthrough can result from small yet effective changes. Only recognized trends will lead to balance, as stated in the verse 75 of TTC

> *Why are people starving?*
> *Because those above them are taxing them too heavily.*
> *That is why they are starving.*
> *Why are the people hard to manage?*
> *Because those above them are fussy and have private ends to serve.*
> *That is why they are hard to manage.*

Zirán in the Course of Events 69

Such critical perspectives especially need to be considered for the self-sufficient comprehension of the contemporary leadership context in developing markets. If you put too much effort on a particular standpoint, there can be a severe risk of neglecting certain aspects that could bring the undertaking to fall. Pursue for certain influences that uncover areas of vulnerability. Adding further considerations of informed wedge opportunities could as well reduce uncertainty and expose related chances.

By understanding the dynamics of markets for considered offerings, one can anticipate favorable situations that show up under the right circumstances. Assured accomplishment depends on the ability to be watchful until those conditions occur. To get on the right path can be rewarding, so long as one can make her own decisions upon consideration of various influencing factors.

Aligned strategy is combining demand and availability of resources to achieve a state of balance. Insightful leaders appreciate talented experts acting in their domain areas. The ability to integrate such contributions to the expected achievements is a gifted skill. To act in flow, a skillful leader with distinct organizational composition skills can effortlessly "*push the boat along with the current*" aiming at empowering like-minded folks. The empowerment of contributors pays back in a multitude of benefits on the road to success. A fair mix of skills and desire for a change motivated around a common purpose is driving such personalities, as it is stated in the verse 47 of TTC

> *Without opening your door, you can know the whole world.*
> *Without looking out your window,*
> *you can understand the way of the Tao.*
> *The more knowledge you seek, the less you will understand.*
> *The Master understands without leaving,*
> *sees clearly without looking,*
> *accomplishes much without doing anything.*

Rather than spending precious time with empirical considerations, experiential regulation of occurrences with the proper utilization of resources at hand could preferably lead to desired results. Contrary to the common belief that addition is always beneficial, reality shows that subtraction as well has its attractions. In fast-moving business environments, the best performance can only be attained with the application of intuitive understanding in recognition of driving forces. At the bottom line, only spending wisely within defined objectives keeps you safe on a strategic path.

When driving business from the core, one can consider available potential to leverage the scope of improvements and scale in growth. Comprehensive understanding of current market conditions will prevent possible misunderstandings from exposition of the outdated business practices. A thorough assessment of the own portfolio would expose its key contributors and allow for reasonable divestment to the core with focus on priorities, leading to improvements in priorities across functions and closer cooperation across the organization. A buy-in from top management to suggestions for improvements can have a positive effect on the processes. Creative leadership considers any feasible advancements in the employee contributions.

> Former SAP's CEO Bill McDermott initiated a *"Driving Simplicity"* program for corporate business processes. From a solid foundation of strengths in business applications, the company has focused on *"Simplicity"* for further expansion of its portfolio. Employees considered the initiatives *"Keep the Promise"*, *"Tell it like it is"*, *"Stay curious"*, *"Build bridges, not silos"*, *"Embrace differences"* as the corporate *"How we Run"* approach. Particularly, the encouragement to *"Tell it like it is"* at every opportunity within a changing environment has strengthened existing abilities. Specifically, it supports an uncluttered mindset for active listening to the intended meaning. In par, *"Stay curious"* has a tendency towards a stronger company culture with shared values at all levels of the global organization.

Organizations act in arrangements of interdependencies and relationships. There are external circumstances in business that are calling for adequate ways to respond in strategy and execution. At any time, new applications can evolve as an outcome of gained insights. How to ensure a positive influence? Personal beliefs make themselves visible by conductive appearing. As adept in problem-solving, we have a repetitive chance to reconsider any setbacks. Occasionally, you might fail to deliver on expected outcome, but even worth it is when you are not following on your promises. Take your time to establish credibility by digesting the statements in the verse 54 of TTC

> *What is firmly set up can't be pulled down;*
> *What is firmly embraced cannot slip free.*
> *And your sons and grandsons, as a result, will sacrifice without end.*
> *When you cultivate it in your person,*
>   *your virtue will then be genuine;*
> *When you cultivate it in your family,*
>   *your virtue will then overflow;*
> *When you cultivate it in your village,*
>   *your virtue will then be long lasting;*
> *When you cultivate it in your state,*
>   *your virtue will then be abundant;*
> *And when you cultivate it throughout the world,*
>   *your virtue will then be widespread.*

Taoism rehearses mutually entailing circles through which the rippling effect of cultivation takes place. Pure motives leave an imprint with repetitive expressions of virtuous behavior. The ability to establish and maintain professional credibility is a vital source of legitimacy on the career path. Any rewards of a high-quality culture are significant within any project execution—success lies in the anticipation and continuous tracking of expectations on all sides—customer, own team, and partners engaged. Sustainable influence has a spreading outward ripple effect in the state of existence of matters.

It's important to learn from the ongoing experimentation to adjust future assumptions through practice. Understanding the circumstances of failed projects or lost deals can be beneficial to business growth. A proper *Loss Analysis* sorts out flaws in internal processes and lays out views of customer requirements. The insights would show where the execution was weak, get support for further engagement, and break any bonds that might hurt the customer relationship.

Propagation of the realized findings can lead to improved products, value proposition, effective sales, and, ultimately, customer satisfaction. Chinese businesspeople often emphasize prevention, as expressed in the synopsis of the verse 52 in TTC

> *To see the small is to have insight.*
> *To hold on to weakness is to be strong.*
> *Use the lights but return to your insight.*
> *Do not bring calamities upon yourself.*
> *This is the way of cultivating the Changeless.*

Application of key principles can prevent from misconduct in business ventures and increase flexibility rooted in the knowledge of how things properly work—lest people be tempted or alarmed.

Keeping profitable positions in big accounts will secure the own budget for the upcoming periods. Kouzes and Posner state in their "Practice 3" that to challenge the process "*You have to become involved, engaged, and curious*" (Kouzes and Posner, 2012). Sometimes leaders can be even perceived as spiritualized beings. It stems from the fact that they try to convey complex interrelationships and possess the ability to negotiate complex situations safely. We try to balance key objectives at stake during negotiations, while assuming a fruitful relationship with our counterpart. Non-pretending leaders treat others in their generous spirit very well—especially those in their networks. Actually, they must do so. Otherwise, they will miss substantial contacts and notable followers. Understanding of circularity and reversion makes them realize the importance and relevance of even minor tasks that can contribute to the constructive accomplishments, as profoundly expressed in the verse 6 of TTC

> *The Tao is called the Great Mother:*
> *empty yet inexhaustible, it gives birth to infinite worlds.*
> *It is always present within you. You can use it any way you want.*

Taoist mindful notions focus attention on the present state. A steady and orderly performance with an open mind constantly leads to favorable outcome. In comparison, a warning of restless activities can also be seen in a reference to the verse 60 in TTC that starts with

> *To **govern larger countries** be **like frying small fish** (cautiously) ...*

Nowadays, office networks cannot keep up with the constantly growing contacts on social media platforms. The later can contribute to the exchange of nonconformist ideas—especially if promoted by opinion leaders characterized above all by their strong loyalty to key principles. Neither fish nor enterprise shall be dissected through too much intervention. Even small changes can result in a big difference.

According to the saying *"To be honest is best"*, understanding of own abilities strengthens self-awareness and supports binds within teams that are sharing common goals. Personal intuition supports an early assessment of the trends, so that with an early intervention, a smooth transition of established processes can be initiated. Only steady activity in accordance with own abilities creates a trustful environment for an effective collaboration—rightly so when team members are coming from a different cultural environment. Involvement from attentive listening requires certitude as a crucial component of collaboration can arise from an open communication with counterparts. Kouzes and Posner "Practice 5" outlines that *"Leaders give heart by visibly recognizing people's contributions to the common vision"* (Kouzes and Posner, 2012).

> In today's highly competitive climate, numerous companies have acknowledged that trust is imperative in *Customer Experience*. All the same, in developing markets it can be confirmed that *trust* among the business partners counts more than terms and conditions of contractual frameworks. One of the stakeholders at my target customer has clearly stated: *"Every deal requires mainly three constituents: the provider, the buyer, and a trustful relationship"*. Clearly, every buyer wants to be treated well. One way at an early stage of business relationships is a *"Letter of Intent"* outlining the initial understanding between the parties. Next could be a *"Proof of concept"* pilot project to clarify on key requirements, or to test the feasibility of business concepts and proposals, prior to providing solutions to problems and implementation of jointly agreed goals.

When dealing with business in turbulent times with dynamic changes happening around us regularly, the statement from Warren Buffett is worth to be followed *"It is impossible to un-sign a contract, so do all your thinking before you sign"* (Buffett & Clark, 2008, p. 8).

Experience truly matters to identify and avoid pitfall traps being laid by your opponents within the negotiation process. Comprehensive and thorough risk review done with the involvement of domain experts and legal advisors can shed light into *troubled waters* in tumultuous times and show ways from a probability of crash occurrence. Getting an *exit clause* into a contract could prevent a possible disaster of a "*bleeding project*". Hence, it helps to internalize the following proposition "*To stay out of trouble, just do the right thing at the right time*".

Any multi-facet assessment of possible pitfalls would increase awareness of critical trends, being articulated as a cautionary counsel in the verse 23 of TTC

> *To rarely speak—such is the way of Nature.*
> *Fierce winds don't last the whole morning.*
> *Torrential rains don't last the whole day.*
> *Who makes these things?*
> *If even Heaven and Earth can't make these last long—*
> *How much the long is this true for man?!*
> *Therefore, one who devotes himself to the Way is one with the Way;*
> *One who devotes himself to Virtue is one with that Virtue;*
> *And one who devotes himself to losing is one with that loss.*
> *To the one who is one with Virtue, the Way also gives Virtue;*
> *While for the one who is with his loss, the Way also disregards him.*

Freedom of decision is based on the insight into the necessity of certain processes. Both nature's way of self-regulation and the natural way of following one's personal truth display similar attainability and effectiveness through thorough awareness of processes. Included warning in the closing is noteworthy.

> *It is only when one does not have enough faith in others*
> *That others will not have faith in him.*

Trust can be expressed as a reciprocal feeling of mutually associated interconnection. Lack of proper nurture in business relationships can result in the loss of personal credibility. Authentic behavior results from conscious reflection of potent cooperative aspirations and deeply felt self-awareness. Surely, there is a requirement of honesty.

There is no shortcut to sincere and proper search for opportunities for the possible improvements. Amazing results of self-fulfilling prophecies certainly comply with the statement from Henry Ford "*Whether you think you can, or you think you can't, you're right*". Successful leaders can regard every encounter as an opportunity for advancement. By repeatedly executing objective reality checks, they avoid becoming ingrown. Coming with a long-term perspective, a contemporary leader can be tolerant of short-term mistakes. Going forward, it pays off to review what is on the right course of affairs, and whether anything is triggering a change.

> Accumulated experience shall be provided across the organization for others to apply and improve. There are several methodological tools that can support development. Only by capturing relevant information, one can foster meaningful communication across teams and divisions. A valid approach is to create templates as a set of standards, where predefined sectors ensure provision of relevant data. In a combination with guiding principles of proven processes in the business life cycle stages, they contribute to the overall success. At initiation, proper matching to similar cases with adjustments to predetermined requirements is of major relevance. Mostly, refined application of tried and tested arrangements contributes to growth. Expansion of established market presence depends on ability for proven repeatable efficient success.

Enforcement of desired solutions when paired with control addiction is inefficient and misleading. None can conceal their beliefs—they become visible in saying and doing. Whatever you decide to apportion the credit for a desirable solution, it depends on several conditions. When could you ask for extraordinary contributions? Classical Taoism values spontaneous behaviors based on internationalized beliefs. Specifically, it acknowledges natural forming within all *open systems*—in management science their property is self-discipline when keeping with throughput of resources from available domains. Interactions lead to patterns, that are to be recognized by instinctive understanding from an extraordinary sense for relevant changes around you. Anything that has happened can't simply not happen. Thus, the main aim is at clarification of the consequences, as divulged in the verse 74 of TTC

> *If you do not fear death, then how can it intimidate you?*
> *If you aren't afraid of dying, there is nothing you cannot do.*
> *Those who harm others are like inexperienced boys*
> *trying to take the place of a great lumberjack.*

Trying to fill his shoes will only get them seriously hurt.

Every action can cause wide-ranging effects. Advanced leaders seek their personal balance in dynamic integration within chosen communities. They anticipate perception of others to create greater understanding and can avoid emergencies with improved awareness and foresight. Collaborative goals and objectives get applied at the level of thought through plans and individual actions. As stated by John Heider "*The wise leader knows that there are natural consequences for every act. The task is to shed light on these, not to attack the behaviour itself*" (Heider, 2015, p. 74).

Attention to the core business of a corporation makes it succeed in a long run. Every enterprise specializes on something that contributes to its compelling advantage and leads to lasting economic gains and growth. New products are often created from the combination of proven components. Based on a company's focus on its unique competitive advantage, further capacities can be developed through partnerships in the framework of in–/outsourcing. Enterprises can certainly consider innovating through outsourcing to gain more market share. The funds and resources that are freed up should rather be used to strengthen core areas. It should be noted that this is not primarily about cost savings because every cooperation leads to an increased effort in communication and coordination.

Company culture, consisting of shared beliefs and attitudes, has an impact on organizational development. As such, the verse 14 in TTC enunciates several aspects of sustainable management.

> *Look, and it can't be seen. Listen, and it can't be heard.*
> *Reach, and it can't be grasped.*
> *Above, it isn't bright. Below, it isn't dark.*
> *Seamless, unnamable, it returns to the realm of nothing.*
> *Form that includes all forms, image without an image,*
> *subtle, beyond all conception.*
> *Approach it and there is no beginning; follow it and there is no end.*
> *You can't know it, but you can be it, at ease in your own life.*
> *Just realize where you come from: this is the essence of wisdom.*

Zirán in the Course of Events

An objective consciousness needs recollection. Being open and receptive in present time affirms ability for enduring development on the path forward. Single senses contribute to intermediate stages in conclusions about actuality. Merging to prevalence, they soar to a next level of abstraction, taking part in rational cognition on the necessities of cyclic changes.

Contemporary leadership styles are necessary for change management. Management ability to combine work duties with personal ideas motivates others to follow. It can be a challenge to get certain conservative progress mavericks into *collaboration*. When properly applied, the verse 10 from TTC can become the bedrock of success with adaptation to long-term development.

> ***Producing and developing, producing without possessing,***
> ***doing without presuming, growing without domineering:***
> ***This is called mysterious power.***

Resolving issues at hand naturally leads to higher confidence in own abilities and greater strengths of peers. By acknowledging their achievements, it's feasible to gain buy-in into joint efforts within ongoing transition to an appropriate state.

It pays off to distinguish effects within hierarchical organizations versus collaboration networks. Hierarchies are well suited to set knowledge-based trends, while networks work well in difficult times, as outlined in the verse 57 of TTC by proposing strength from being straightforward, crafty but not meddlesome without conscious unity of purpose.

> ***Hence, wise men advise: I act without intervening,***
> ***and yet*** *the people by itself* ***becomes transformed;***
> ***I prefer stillness, and yet*** *the people by itself* ***becomes of integrity;***
> ***I act without busyness, and yet*** *the people by itself* ***becomes enriched;***
> ***I am without desire, and yet*** *the people by itself* ***becomes simple.***

Inspiring leaders enable empowered staff in a non-authoritarian manner with a surrounding congenial to self-realization within natural conditions. The domination of knowledge denotes advantage that serves to secure a position of authority—it goes back to a somewhat outdated understanding of "*knowledge is power*" that gradually diminishes with the era of social and market-related transparency.

It certainly helps to be aware of own strengths and weaknesses. In uncertain situations, people appreciate exceptional ability to identify a viable solution to the given challenge—especially, if it is in line with coordinated efforts. Their motivation on contractual obligations' attainment can raise, provided there are clear statements in the joint agreement. As expressed in the verse 79 of TTC, everybody depends on the fulfillment of the agreed obligations.

> *Great grudge once appeased, certainly there is a rest of resentment;*
> *how could that accordingly serve as 'make good' again?*
> *Therefore, wise men hold the left side of contracts,*
> *but not claiming from others.*
> *With Inner Power, you keep contracts,*
> *without Inner Power you stand on demands.*

As such, even failures can be treated as an opportunity. In ancient China, contracts were written on "tally"–like bamboo sticks, the *left* side for the creditor, the *right* for the debtor. The leader in the spirit of the *TAO*, can, if necessary, take over both sides by the means of their unrestricted *TE* and even refuse to collect debatable claims.

Qì in Cyclic Innovation

*"Creativity is thinking up new things.
Innovation is doing new things".* Theodore Levitt

Most combined product or process innovations are greater than their parts. The interdisciplinary impact of research and development is above average in the contribution to competitive advantage over rivals. In addition to impact-driven innovation activities, institutional value management can support decision-making that will impact long-term earnings. With impact comes responsibility. Let's review in this section the meaning of cyclical approach to energetic leadership and its implications for management. In Chinese, *qi* stands for interrelation of energy patterns. On the next pages, we are going to see how energy is driving the circle of change and examine how structures that effectively sustain during ongoing business cycles.

Innovation is at best combining creativity with conception. Based on the underlying character of the business, one can gain exclusivity in offerings from *thought leadership* that is about novel and potentially winning courses of action. Introducing revolutionary products to the markets as a first mover is a fair chance for a superior position. The window of opportunity to capitalize on innovation is slim, though, before rivalry emerges from imitations of key functions that can be combined with further capabilities. Driven by the demanding needs of customers, only tight cross-functional integration and pioneering process improvements can reduce the risk of innovation failures. What share of revenue shall be allocated to research and development efforts? It's worth considering, whether these costs depend on excess cash or rely on an infusion of capital. Any further examination of complementary assets as further capabilities to support the commercialization of a technological innovation could as well be considered as a winning strategy.

Sometimes, innovation can be confrontation with the established actuality. Addressing the continuous complexity and frequent changes in business application scenarios, smart enterprises are considering the *Cyclic Innovation Model* (CIM)[1] that combines technological and business sectors closely intertwined with their markets considering input from the science in the circle of change. For a mega-project, outstanding contributions of the area experts with resources across several countries and business lines require extraordinary efforts in proactive management. An involvement of external experts could uncover hidden talents within the existing workforce that leads even more to a need for dynamic adaptation of business processes. Technological development has enabled individuals and corporations to influence processes on a larger scale. Every business interaction depends on many factors. Suppliers, products, and needs of interested parties are constantly being reshuffled. It would

---

[1] https://www.toolshero.com/innovation/berkhout-cyclic-innovation-model-cim/.

be fatally hasty to draw general conclusions from individual cases. Only scaling strategies ensure multiple developments. Finding the most relevant sources of information for your undertaking can be a mixture of science and art.

Joseph Schumpeter (1883–1950), as one of the most influential economists of the early twentieth century, has identified innovation as the critical dimension of economic change. He argued that it revolves around innovation, certain entrepreneurial activities, and overall market power. Taoism claims that there are underlying forces that leave nothing unattained. Let's probe a message from the verse 16 in TTC

> *By knowing the constant we can accept things as they are.*
> *By accepting things as they are, we become impartial.*

It is about responsibility for the continuation of established best practices, while consistency can be reached from harmonization. The leader is receptive to the ongoing events without bias, anticipating common imperatives resulting from high-yielding dialog arising from clear reasoning with relevant response.

A combination of organizational objectives with personalized views ensures comprehensive understanding of required steps toward reaching desired goals. On occasions, one can also secure own income by turning customers into partners. It's far better to also include strategic partners into the best of breed win–win–win relationship, where every party contributes to the overall attainment. "*You may say I'm a dreamer, but I'm not the only one. I hope someday you'll join us and the world will be as one*".[2] This can only work if each party is ready to share its strategies with others in common arrangement. Your competitors might present an attractive value proposition at any time. The complement providers benefit from joint strategies in offering bundled goods or supplementary services. Competitive advantage can be increased through subscription maintenance models.

---

[2] Refrain in the song "Imagine" by John Lennon.

> Such an approach is realized by start-up companies that look for a market niche they can enter by providing new solutions to uncovered needs. One of the rationales could be that their prototypes could require fine-tuning for application of the customer needs, as well as proper packaging with 3rd party offerings. In such a constellation, every party contributes with fair share to the overall solution. A tricky point though is clarification of the "intellectual property" attribution and agreement on the further sale of that bundle. A significant number of innovative products could expose similar conditions.

The pressures for accelerated continuous innovations increase with enhanced customer demands. A new idea leads to actions in several directions—from market analysis and product specification to consulting work. Often, it requires persuasion to turn a viable idea into execution. New opportunities can be developed only from a compound attention. Leaders know how to subdue obstacles to disruptive corporate innovations. Their determination in the transformational innovation can encourage others to act.

Any innovative approach needs endorsement of supportive general or functional managers, depending on their sphere of responsibility, with a conscious follow through on commitments to incurring change. One needs to consider broader implications along the value chain for the intention of win–win–win situations applicable for individuals, corporations, and the environment.

A strong ability to adaptation often enables greater expansion and occupation of niche markets with untapped potential yet reasonable profit margins. Among key aspects considered for the new initiatives are continuously raising needs of defined target groups. Focus on core competencies is the proper way to success, starting from proactively creating opportunities and turning them into new realities. The traditional German breweries now producing craft beer, or the renewed northern Italian textile industry, can serve as examples.

The statement "*the future is now*" is valid more than ever, while our present is ephemeral. The past is the foundation for possible futures. To prospect possibilities, one needs to consciously attend to the present conditions. With a reference to relevant topics covered in the previous encounters, you can demonstrate attention to detail in a wider range of possibilities, as indicated in the verse 18 of TTC

> **When the Great Way is deserted, then there is humanitarian duty.**
> **When intelligence comes forth, there is great fabrication.**
> **When relations are discordant, then there is family love.**
> **When the national polity is benighted and confused,**
> **then there are loyal ministers.**

An overall meaning lies in the adaptation of John Heider, "*once you leave the path of simple consciousness, you enter the labyrinth of cleverness, competition, and imitation*" (Heider, 2015, p. 18)—mainly because its realization binds resources. A successful company is best in harmony with the environment in which it operates. With any explicit determination for the implementation of a promising idea, one implicitly lets several other options becoming neglected.

Quite often, career ambitions can depend on the support of a sponsor. Alternatively, with the clearly established criteria, it can be worth effort introducing a role of a *champion* with the clear ambition to establish a path to personal growth by improving further capabilities.

> At the company leading in business applications, the performance champions are encouraged to apply for a temporary fellowship within other divisions or locations. That offering creates the ability to learn new topics and uncover other ways of collaboration. To achieve the extraordinary, multidisciplinary teams can explore entrepreneurial initiatives with a diverse mix of cultures and experience levels. They collect ideas from discussions, participate in online forums, or contribute to virtual sessions. The assigned coordinators can function as a link to functional experts, creating fruitful conditions for exchange and feedback. For instance, several years ago, we could establish a dedicated *"Big data"* initiative by creating specific use cases from cogent case studies. It clearly paid off with improvements of sales plays and reasoned implementation guidelines.

> In a climate of constant innovation and transformation, companies culture needs to support creativity, while also considering risks from changing

> processes. New offerings get coupled with the core competencies to improve the possible revenue streams. Utilizing innovative approaches, the corporation continuous to perform gratifyingly as well in new and changing markets.

It requires certain belief and persistence to conjure and pursue ideas. No one knows all possible progressive outcomes, as it is effectively impossible to determine to what extent multiple causes contribute to effects. Progressive leaders are ready to depart from inherited conventions. When is it worth helping creativity to break through? An ingenuity free of limiting preconceptions is impetus to innovative approach, always best under considerations of the economic realities—certainly, those who don't follow fundamental economics are going to perform poorly. Surely, this principle is spurring us to attend to neglected problems, as outlined with examples in the next paragraph.

A prime example of short-sighted enterprise behavior is IBM's inability to realize the potential of personal computers back in the 1980s—which actually has enabled the growth of Microsoft. Genuine leadership development is a long-term endeavor. It must foresee the trends and be ready for a radical change if/s it is required to maintain and further develop market position. The leading Enterprise Application company remains persistent with its multi-facet Cloud strategy. On that path, its hybrid offerings aid customers in the transformation. Accordingly, Professional Services departments are carefully preventing so-called *bleeding projects* by conducting formal bid reviews and applying thorough risk mitigation. Hybrid systems exhibit both continuous and discrete dynamic behavior. Applying Internet of things, the manufacturer *Kaeser Compressors* have successfully optimized its business model: next to manufacturing, the company has been targeting eroding profits from traditional products with the new "*Air as a Service*" offering. As such, open innovation can be applied under any business conditions.

Don't miss looking for curiosity around you to see if and how it can be addressed with your suggestions reflecting anticipated demands. If there is a high potential for development of a candidate toward extraordinary growth ambitions, a matching mentor with relevant skills can be the best option. Anticipation of a foreign country is often charged with ideas that are derived from our own cultural aspects. Unfortunately, there are limitations in the understanding of complexity in the economic and political mechanisms of a foreign society we intend to enter. Political processes introduce changes by the means of laws and regulations, which in turn can significantly constrain operations of business organizations. Look, for instance, at the changes from the deregulation in the energy industry that is bringing threads to a few giants as well as chances for many new business models. How do you feel, finding that preferences are against your recommendation? I.e., consider adding weighting to the options at hand.

Truly innovative enterprises encourage establishment of communication channels in a horizontal ecosystem to avoid information distortion. Arguments are most effective when expressed in the language of their target audience. From the outset, pioneering leaders need ways for communication of the characteristics in the desired future state, while managers should overcome silo barriers by expanding their contacts across the broader organization. They encourage employees for cross-departmental projects and beyond. Knowing what to abandon, one can leave any corresponding actions to chance.

> It's a great experience to participate in the development of a start-up company in the business of an information system for healthcare. Driven by a curious and flexible workforce, it is reviving to introduce digital healthcare, covering needs from general practitioners up to the overall healthcare system of a country. We have been working on a broad set of new applications, such as a new health record system *LifeSensor* to combine personal health with medical data, modular *Professional Exchange Server* (incl. *Master Patient Index*) to interconnect general practitioners with clinics, etc. The company focused on managed care organizations (HMOs, ACOs, hospitals), and on the life science industry (pharmaceuticals, med tech) networks. We closely worked in cooperation with providers of healthcare solutions and services. As an integrating *eHealth Platform* the personalized health suite could be used worldwide by selectively assigning access to physicians as required. Differing from the practices of an established company, a start-up depends on a frequent update of its business plan addressing expectations of investors.

Innovation contributes to advancement. Innovative enterprises are seeking ways to improve and be acknowledged for thought leadership. It can be disseminated by the means of topical *"white papers"*, proven *"best practices"*, as well as keynote speeches in prestigious events. Exemplary thought leaders foster conditions for creativity, defining clear objectives for growth. Their ability to consider *more* important from *less* relevant is necessary for a decision to *take or leave* under given circumstances. The quest is on how to promote new possibilities. It's worth trying new approaches, experimenting with available assets, learn from errors and gradually move ahead into desired direction. The verse 4 in TTC outlines certain requirements needed to cope with uncertainty.

> *The Way is unimpeded harmony;*
> *its potential may never be fully exploited.*
> *It is as deep as the source of all things;*
> *it blunts the edges, resolves the complications,*
> *harmonizes the light, assimilates to the world.*
> *Profoundly still, it seems to be there:*
> *I don't know whose child it is, before the creation of images.*

Creativity can often follow a spontaneous experience. The faculty of an idea is as such the bearing of the possibilities of its realization.

Our world can be viewed in complementary polarities, as utterly pointed out with many insights by Daniel Kahneman[3] in his work "thinking, fast, and slow". Any decision-making requires both qualities, rational evaluation, and intuitive capture of a given situation, while markets are changing in a *yang* attitude of effort and *yin* manner of reception within ongoing impermanence. The Chinese principle of *yang* as activity and *yin* as deliberation goes beyond binary representation. Originating from depiction of a bright and dark sides of a hill that varies throughout the day (or night) depending on the position of the sun (or moon) these phenomena can equally be viewed by the means of ideas and execution, proper initiation and timely completion, meaningful differentiation and integration, reasonable order and delivery, etc. By any over-determined focusing, both antipodes (polarities) take turns

---

[3] In 2002, he was awarded the Nobel Memorial Prize in Economic Sciences.

in the structural leading and managing others or own affairs within a variety of contexts, as expressed in the verse 2 of TTC

> *When the people of the world all know beauty as beauty,*
> *there arises the recognition of ugliness.*
> *When they all know the good as good,*
> *there arises the recognition of evil.*
> *Therefore:*
> *Being and non-being produce each other;*
> *Difficult and easy complete each other;*
> *Long and short contrast each other;*
> *High and low distinguish each other;*
> *Front and back follow each other.*

A visionary leader can see unity in the reversal between opposites. An extreme attention to one side (feature, aspect, position) can lead to awareness of the other side both in human intellectual capacity and emotional consciousness. It could be gained by practiced empathy with sensitivity to the critical requirements and differentiated recognition in awareness of opposite points of view.

In order to secure a healthy business growth, it's essential to identify the driving and restraining forces of change. Keeping up with the markets, any challenges are inextricably linked to new possibilities. For quite some time, my favorite motto has been the statement by an American industrialist Henry J. Kaiser, *"problems are only opportunities in work clothes"*. Taoism encourages forward-thinking behavior with disclosure of factors that lead to lesser activity than addressing problems due to unacceptable misjudgment. The verse 44 in TTC articulates a great suggestion to be simply open-minded and to act, as often as possible, non-judgmental.

> *Fame or health—which is more dear?*
> *Your health or possessions—which is worth more?*
> *Gain or loss—in which is there harm?*
> *If your desires are great, you're bound to be extravagant;*
> *If you store much away, you're bound to lose a great deal.*
> *Therefore, if you know contentment, you'll not be disgraced.*
> *If you know when to stop, you'll suffer no harm.*
> *And in this way you can last a very long time.*

Be assured that your contributions to success will get noticed. Good reputation is a very valuable resource, especially in business conduct. It is based upon carrying out your promises—hard to gain, yet easy to shed. Big corporations expand from so-called "*inner security*" as confidence in the ability to grow and strengthen their presence from coherent execution.

Any decision we make is either fact-based or intuitive, and most often, it constitutes a combination of both attributes. Constant adaption to change is the norm for a leader in business applications.

> To further strengthen its leading position in the enterprise application market, SAP has acquired key players in distinct areas, incl. Business Objects for Business Intelligence applications, Sybase for technology and business solutions, Ariba for improved procurement process, SuccessFactors for human capital management, Fieldglass for vendor management, and Concur for travel and expense management services. Such strategy is clearly showing respect for the achievements of these companies by ensuring an overall value creation from the aggregation of best possible by-products by fully integrating the acquired companies with creation of viable multi-business models around distinctive competencies. These acquisitions brought further innovations that enable SAP to become a cloud-based enterprise with a unique integrated offering for its customers.

Taking note of the increasing complexity, good governance relies on authentic cooperation within established guidelines, leading to sustainable growth. We should not mistake met agreements for truth, even if ratified by several parties involved. Best decisions are made based on trusted experience, which comes from practice. To gain a mastery of fortune, confidence levels content with own knowledge of factors for successful execution—and not on opinions. Stronger effects can result from repeated use. Sometimes, though, the abundance of ambitions can reach out beyond current capabilities.

It's best to have meaningful business calls or conduct fruitful meetings when being relaxed and confident on the subject to pursue distinctive competencies. All and sundry deserve outside confirmation of their abilities and encouragement for further efforts. To get convinced on proven knowledge, frequent rehearsal of own ideas upon changing circumstances pays off. Most people appreciate if they experience their aid being recognized as a valuable contribution to the overall strategy.

It requires a counterpoint to induce harmonious patterns. A flawless execution has become the resounding pattern of modern business, linking present goals with outcomes by the meaning of *key performance indicators* (*KPIs*) adjusted within operating planning to monitor and secure available strengths. Established metrics provide information about future outcomes. KPIs shape the work culture and thus permeate the thinking and norms of employees. Taking care of their needs ensures their loyalty to the company. Performance measurements on KPI-related indexes that support strategic priorities can spark discussions toward improvements. Honest review of alternative solutions to critical issues can be addressed with rapport as "*is a close and harmonious relationship in which quality people or groups concerned are "in sync" with each other, understand each other's feelings or ideas, and communicate smoothly*".[4]

Classical Taoism fosters the idea of a cyclically organized world—acting without any final purpose. With systematic research and critical analysis, clear aspirations for desirable outcome shall get to the top list of priorities. Creative cross-industry system providers know how to discover needs that have not yet manifested themselves and to satisfy them with innovative solutions.

Leadership is an ongoing effort in changing, evolving from innovation, and developing with support from contributors. The verse 71 in TTC clarifies on a thorough understanding of any shortages with complementing solutions.

> *To know you don't know is best.*
> *Not to know you don't know is a flaw.*
> *Therefore, the Sage's not being flawed*
> *Stems from his recognizing a flaw as a flaw.*
> *Therefore, he is flawless.*

A variety of interests can bring natural resistance to the perceived impressions of enforced influence. In business discussions, we are usually

---

[4] See https://en.wikipedia.org/wiki/Rapport.

concerned with quantities, often neglecting qualitative facets. A crucial skill relies on the ability to analyze matters and carry out pertinent actions based on the investigation. When we identify failings and evenly learn from them, they start loosing negative effects.

We come to evaluate adaptation topics around *being* and *doing* in the following chapter, where we can also review the impact of cyclical business disruptions.

Jing in Dynamic Adaptation

"Don't find fault, find a remedy". Henry Ford

Nothing in business stands still, as it is continuously driven by ever-changing markets and new technology. Our daily activities consist of active choices. We cannot only react by continuously evolving to change in our environment. Instead, we shall look for the essential improvements in operations, aiming at possible contributions in securing cash flow. In this section, we shall review some of the key contributing factors. Anticipating a particular challenge begins with finding ways to overcome its limiting factors. Among essential drivers can be balanced appreciation of agility and integrity. Don't underestimate the purpose of "*good practices*" derived from lessons learned to see how they can fit under certain preconditions, which can secure long-term efficiency upon overcoming resistance of current processes. On such foundations, it is congenial to co-creatively develop and exchange new ideas across the enterprise.

Adaptability is sometimes delineated by acceptance of or resistance to an ongoing change. Numerous outside interests might be essential factors in establishing a base for business success in a new environment. In the era of geopolitics, the ability to flexibly overcome regional crises is crucial. When realizing a disbalance between the well-defined goals and occurring obstacles, it might be indispensable to halt and impose situational awareness for necessary adjustments. The effectiveness of the objective management under the conditions of ongoing environmental changes depends on timely response. Perception of time goes beyond pure quantitative measures, and it can also be of a qualitative (before/after, ongoing, ready state) nature.

One can surely concede that "*successful companies are communities of purpose*". Hierarchical structures established within corporate structures could affect creative contributions from business area teams that are interlinked within dynamic networks. Employees can usually associate themselves with a group within a structure. Simply by emphasizing major achievements of highlighted individuals within divisions, companies can validate the flow of arguments. With such assignment of the credit arises a notion of a generalized "*we*" against "*them*" tendency, with commitment to the overall objectives—taking into considerations common value creation for customers.

Conscious leaders promote integrity, with attention to opposite positions. Consciousness works by clarifying constraints while also pragmatically harmonizing conflicts, as proposed in the verse 56 of TTC.

> **Be like the Tao. It can't be approached or withdrawn from, benefited or harmed, honoured or brought into disgrace. It gives itself up continually. That is why it endures.**

To avoid a clash of cultures, be aware that your counterparts in the international business could assume inherent promises that may be common in their cultural context but are at first unknown to you.

> One of the CEE countries has been a "white spot" for the enterprise I worked for in a function of a business development manager. My initial win there was based on successful participation in a World Bank tender. For the implementation project, we could recruit a local services company as a partner. It went well until the enhanced pipeline made it necessary to consider parallel sourcing with another local company that could offer specific skills to target industries. This move has created anxiety at the initial partner on the market share, even if related conditions were clearly stated in our joint business plan. He started sending blackmailing notes, and it became necessary to get legal counsel for support. Was there anything we could have done to prevent his conniving acting? With the long-term perspective, we cannot fulfill expectations of certain individuals, just as we can't accept the aftermath of an extraordinary behavior.

Entering emerging markets, enterprises can get a head start on their competition. For most businesses, assured growth within the initial stage of market entry will be no easy feat. Within economies of scale, hurdles are set up efforts, regulatory obstacles, and the sociocultural character of the target country—as we have seen in the examples above. The right conditions could be precarious. Introduction of products requires additional efforts, as implementation essentially depends on the contributions of local resources involved. At times, one needs a "*staying power*" because it can take time for new business practices to prove themselves. How to establish and secure a healthy growth for your corporation? Affected by several hard to be foreseen factors, overall growth rate can decline and profits level out—despite innovative and exemplary offerings. No infusion of funds can withhold the inevitable, as has been emphasized in the verse 67 of TTC

> *Some say that my teaching is nonsense.*
> *Others call it lofty but impractical.*
> *But to those who have looked inside themselves,*
> *this nonsense makes perfect sense.*

> *And to those who put it into practice,*
> *this loftiness has roots that go deep.*
> *I have just three things to teach: simplicity, patience, compassion.*
> *These three are your greatest treasures.*
> *Simple in actions and in thoughts,*
> *you return to the source of being.*
> *Patient with both friends and enemies,*
> *you accord with the way things are.*
> *Compassionate toward yourself, you reconcile all beings in the world.*

Established knowledge states that capital expenses are usually front-loaded but can be reduced by profound actions. The necessity of continuous adoption is simply reality. Patience leads to generosity, while compassion, especially when together with a true humility, "*is Key to Good Leadership in Business Management*".[1]

An open attitude to outside expertise paired with elaboration of local thought leaders can be observed in *Kazakhstan*. This country has been awarded in 2020 as the number one across the globe for protecting minority investors' rights. Despite the ongoing China-Russia vicinity, this country pursues fruitful partnerships with enterprises worldwide. The contemporary conditions of a transit economy call for flexibility in transformational leadership skills.

> The *Alma-Ata Declaration* expressed the need for purposeful operations by governments, health and development workers, and the world community to protect and promote the health of all people. Serving its multinational population spread across vast territory, the Kazakh government has initiated a broad training program for its candidates for leadership roles. Under the leadership of Deloitte's Life Sciences and Health Care group, we could conduct a series of fruitful meetings for successful collaboration with the local players aiming at improvements in the health system across this country.

---

[1] https://blog.peoplefirstps.com/connect2lead/leadership-business-management.

> The *Karachaganak Field* is one of the world's largest gas condensate fields. In 1992, Eni and British Gas were awarded negotiating rights, forming a partnership company. Following on, American Chevron Corp. and Russian Lukoil signed with them and the Kazakhstan government a 40-year sharing agreement to develop the field for world markets. This agreement has been consolidated under Karachaganak Petroleum Operating company.

> Working with the *National Bank*, we noticed a significant lag between an agreement for implementation and activation of required resources. At the level of the regional office, we had to temporarily establish a flexible bonus plan for the local sales and services staff to balance off rigid limitations at the level of global HR policies.

Best decisions are made by consensus. An extraordinary manager needs to identify a lever toward achievements of defined objectives and, if required, reach out for adjustments in strategies. As for an ideal leader, we could subsist with the meaning of ingenuity and imagination by the means of avoiding tough competition.

> It has been striking to experience severe competitiveness within and across its plants at an industry giant, albeit its rather alternative platforms have been offered to the markets. Such anxiety among staff clearly limits the full potential of possible achievements.

> My next employer promoted a "multivendor architecture" at the core of its system, eliminating any favoritism with the intention to serve every customer equally. It was remarkable how different parts of the international enterprise (software development, sales and marketing, services and support, and others) could best perform as distinct but united organs of a common body.

The dynamic nature of new leads and fulfillment of obligations frequently requires balancing. Due to Wing-Tsit Chan, Taoism expresses aspirations in "*taking no action that is contrary to nature—in other words, letting nature take its own course*". Yet, that does not prevent individuals from attaining their subjectivity in taking autonomous actions, preferably if they are in line with natural course.

> At an expansion deal, we experienced an issue when a holding was convinced to share some licenses with its new acquisition in a country where we did not have any services staff for implementation. I've hired a local project coordinator who turned up to be a friend of the key sponsor there. They expected extra fees for a smooth introduction of new capabilities, which was not put into the equation. We had to reach clarification with the involvement of higher management. If all your actions can be attested, get ready to present your case with unassailable integrity to explicit rules and implicit values of your business conduct. Could we have seen this coming? Some emerging markets are known for poor contracting liabilities. Local companies could change their commitments after initial investments have been made and try to take their trade-off advantage accordingly. With the proven stronghold at the top-level, we could maintain our company reputation without any compromise. Ultimately, we had to control our relationship with these individuals to the benefit of our overall business contemplation within developing markets.

Rapid development technologies support flexible creation of higher quality products addressing customer requirements. Adaptive changes contain incite adoption to new realities by considering any failures due to specific circumstances. When they have occurred, it is recommended to conduct route-cause analysis, and going forward, watch out for similar situations. *Resilience* in business has evolved with influence from the theories of the adaptive capacity and systems dynamics. It's about the personal ability to bounce back from mistakes or even failure. Managers focus on value creation for a multitude of stakeholders (business counterpart, decision makers, partners, or suppliers), while leaders also create broader value that enables systems resilience to be built and maintained.

Any change in organizational processes depends on the fulfillment of preconditions. Knowing how tendencies evolve provides a leader with the powerful position, as stated in the verse 62 of TTC

> *The Way is the pivot of all things:*
> *The treasure of good people, the safeguard of those who are not good.*
> *Fine words can be sold, honoured acts can oppress people;*
> *why should people who are not good abandon them?*
> *Therefore, to establish an emperor and set up high officials,*
> *one many have a great jewel and drive a team of horses,*
> *but that is not as good as advancing calmly on this Way.*
> *Why did the ancients value this Way?*
> *By it one can attain without long seeking*
> *and escape from the faults one has;*
> *therefore it is valued by the world.*

Sustainable processes can unfold naturally—yet we always need to take care of nature. Since 2018, an era of "*ecological civilization*" has been written into the Chinese constitution as the final goal of social and environmental reform within a new society. In Chinese, humility is related to open-mindedness. Deliberate leaders can express their directions with the courage of conviction, yet without pretense. By transcending rational patterns, they don't shy away from fruitful transformation of regulative norms.

We all benefit from the achievements of a competitive market. However, quite often, the impression of stability is a delusion. In market dynamics, continuous change is iterative and vigorous. What if, after reaching agreement, severe disruptions occur? The disruptive world is volatile, uncertain, complex, and ambiguous (VUCA). As we constantly navigate through change, a great deal of turbulence can be brought about by market pressures. Agile processes can better meet the increasing uncertainty of rapidly changing business requirements with considerations of external and internal options. There is always a human side in any business relationship. People prefer to buy time and again from people that they trust the most. Sharing a common business vision with personal encouragement contributes to stronger ties.

> It has been fortunate for me to manage interpersonal rapport with the new CIO of a leading telecommunications company. He was about to

> introduce innovative solutions supporting managed growth of the enterprise. We looked at possible improvements in the areas of financial consolidation, marketing operations, and sales organization. As his ambitions were not fully backed by the supervisory board, we rather agreed to focus on the encompassing revenue assurance and got approval for such a gradual change. And that adjustment put us into an advanced position ahead of the competition.

Academic circles have been investigating into differences between "*Chinese ways of management*" and "*ways of management in China*". We can assume some general and ever-lasting principles of leadership and successful management practices. The concept of *empathy* was found to be a strong factor of ethical behavior in the *Leadership Effectiveness Analysis*™ done by the Management Research Group—it was even one of the three strongest predictors of executive effectiveness. The foreseen importance of empathy within a business context, especially if applied at the right level, is an emerging trend.

An explication of empathy is the ability to uncover something meaningful in your counterpart. We could get others to move from their comfort zone only with appropriate enthusiasm and passion. Kouzes and Posner "Practice 2" suggests that "*if you're going to lead, you have to recognize that your enthusiasm and expressiveness are among your strongest allies in your efforts to generate commitment in others*" (Kouzes and Posner, 2012).

When losing the ability to follow "*the flow of life*", we try to control or even dominate its course. However, only those who adapt will succeed in the long term. An adaptive organization combines meaningful imagination and creative sense. Taoism emphasizes continuity and cyclical development within process efficiency. It cultivates balanced flow and refers to water as a synthesizing image, soft, and powerful, moving with the tranquil times and yielding to natural changes, as stated in the opening of the verse 8 in TTC

> *The supreme good is like water,*
> *which nourishes all things without trying to.*
> *It is content with the low places that people disdain.*
> *Thus it is like the Tao.*

In dwelling, live close to the ground.
In thinking, keep to the simple.
In conflict, be fair and generous.
In governing, don't try to control.
In work, do what you enjoy.
In family life, be completely present.
When you are content to be simply yourself
and don't compare or compete, everybody will respect you.

It's best to exploit natural tendencies instead of pushing on a certain course. With an unrestricted readiness and availability to flow everywhere, water is always adapting to its external environment. For both, water and guidance, the intrinsic core of collaboration is unsalable. Good business practices are premised on honest competence and select expertise bringing initiated matters to a conclusion, while their unforced actuation relies on binding spirit and proper timing.

Failures often result from an underestimation of hidden assumptions—there can be a geographical shift in sourcing, or an acquisition might require certain skills for execution. With mergers and acquisitions, the robust executive team benefits from collaborative skills. Building on networks to explore new market potential, some close alliances could be denoted with joint flexible business planning. A notion of the ability for adaptation to ambiguous changes with strategic adjustments by subtle powers is clearly outlined in the verse 43 of TTC

That which offers no resistance, overcomes the hardest substances.
That which offers no resistance can enter where there is no space.
Few in the world can comprehend the teaching without words,
or understand the value of non-action.

Yielding interventions can bypass severe oppositions. There should be no hesitance to review even a well-thought strategy with revisions according to the ongoing changes in the business conditions. Conscious leaders know that small, yet appropriate, steps can lead to sensible results.

Expressed by R. L. Stevenson, *"everyone lives by selling something"*. There is a strong belief that sales skills have universal application for any business position. Every employee shall contribute to expense recovery. Proactively selling is commonly perceived as a contact game. To appraise any difficult situation, account managers could begin with the numerous outside-in views up to the decisive judgment. It is a gradual difference if you are "*selling to*" somebody, or whether they are "*buying from*" you what they consider necessity. While selling a solution has a generic meaning, the "Solution Selling" methodology as a brand denotes distinct characteristics.[2] Part of the high art in sales is taking into considerations particular interests of members in the *buying center* (resp. "*inner circle*") when they decide whether to purchase your products. In most enterprises, there are only a few personalities who exert influence over strategic purchases.

Creation of new offerings could be done cooperatively with customers. It is prudent to identify sponsors for each feasible alternative within your contribution. Effective measures could reflect capabilities of your offering that contribute to customer's increase in revenue and profits. Yet intangible benefits, such as brand image, or improved employee morale shall also not be underestimated.

> Reviewing the ranking of corporations by industry, it's striking how often the top level is reluctant to a constant change—mostly afraid to slip down from an excellent position and endanger their leadership position. Companies in the mid-range are more open for optimization that can lead them into growth patterns. Hence, when building a sales pipeline, my prime focus has been at the 3rd company in the top-down ranking by industry. By having already reached a fairly good position, they are determined to grow by excellence and are open to gain leadership by innovation—as outlined above.

Effective strategic account management is key for large-scale ventures. Proactive management establishes a sense of responsibility with follow-through on any initiated projects. Aiming at value creation, it is constantly matching detected needs with proven best practices. There is an ongoing series of opportunities. Challenges induce creative individuals interested to overcome any obstacles, ideally under outright considerations of related risks. The ability to adapt lessons from past

---

[2] Sketched out on https://en.wikipedia.org/wiki/Solution_selling.

situations to current needs is rare. The verse 11 of TTC features intrinsic values for anyplace of interrelations.

> *We join spokes together in a wheel,*
> *but it is the centre hole that makes the wagon move.*
> *We shape clay into a pot,*
> *but it is the emptiness inside that holds whatever we want.*
> *We hammer wood for a house,*
> *but it is the inner space that makes it livable.*
> *We work with being, but non-being is what we use.*

In Chinese dialectical reasoning, being 無 and non-being 有 have equal veracity—they are complementary sides in the presence of anything. With the understanding of the benefits of being (quantity) and the functionality of non-being (quality), we can gain advantage from of the unity of opposites.

It could be worth igniting some innovative projects within remote geographies upon discernment of the relationships across business entities. There are several aspects to be considered for a successful large account management as contribution to top and bottom lines revenues. Large enterprises often employ dedicated global account executives assigned to the most important international corporations among their customers. When outlining targets and execution strategies, they also try to appreciate industry trends and particular market conditions. Remarkably, it is easier to receive required attention at a subsidiary, if you come with a recommendation from a larger entity.

From time to time, it's worth considering a change in the business conduct. Under certain circumstances, there is a need to create a new package combining the products used, business advisory services and supporting maintenance. The *services* business organizations usually distinguish between *fixed-price* and *time-and-materials* contractual agreements. Each model has its *pro's* and *con's*, as far as one can define an exit strategy within the risk management considerations, as briefly implied in the verse 32 of TTC

> *Naming is a necessity for order, but naming cannot order all things.*
> *Naming often makes things impersonal,*
> *so we should know when naming should end.*

Knowing when to stop naming, you can avoid the pitfall it brings.

Prosperous managers don't let tempting new undertakings divert their devotion to the completion of the initiated projects. Responding appropriately to proven regulations, they try to stick with the direction taken. This kind of determination contributes to predictability of expected results and is highly appreciated by stakeholders.

It could be a viable approach to consider reimbursable contracts where one gets rewarded on the completion of milestones. Agility and flexibility as a source of strength can as well overcome intense opposition. Versatility in the approach can require a booster for assigned product or project managers in charge of delivering on the company commitments under unexpected circumstances. We can benefit from an agreed course of actions in a unity of shared values.

Global enterprises offer intercultural training to their managers. Joint errands outside formal meetings create space for interpersonal encounters supporting mutual understanding. The verse 59 in TTC is on openness to overcome stereotypes and outdated pattern of actions.

*There is nothing better than moderation
for teaching people or serving Heaven.
Those who use moderation are already on the path to the Tao.
Those who follow the Tao early will have an abundance of virtue.
When there is an abundance of virtue,
there is nothing that cannot be done.*

Some perceive the world as a constructed expectation that comes to fruition of coexistence upon favorable circumstances. There is a call for the ability to unlearn certain fundamental patterns. It can create new realities, as it has been exemplified by a German coach and strategist with cases by categories.[3]

Learning and development are increasingly conveyed in a networked fashion. Rather than applying rigid training curricula, simulation of connected work environment serves better the needs of *digital natives*. Generation Z became influential due to their prevailing virtual connectedness. They are used to consuming more media online than offline and

---

[3] Outlined in https://www.unlearn.eu/en.

prefer a *home-office* setting. Valuing authenticity high, they look for innovative ideation, expect feedback, and recognition within company-wide collaboration processes.

Exemplary leaders accept accountability for changes they impose. An ambiguous strategy is laid between long-term qualitative goals with quantifiable midterm objectives and short-term dynamic planning of distinct activities scheduled toward expected accomplishments. Thorough planning means orientation toward a desired outcome with considerations of the required steps in that direction. When times get difficult, people start looking at how to keep matters in perspective. Hence, it's best to surrender yourself to own limits by providing more room for dynamic adaptation, most obvious resistance could be prevented. Any side effects and potential consequences thereof shall be considered ahead of pursuing long-term perspectives. Event-oriented dynamic adaptation with clarity of desire shall be treated as a gift. Agreed milestones boost focus and ensure pace toward expected progress, allowing for corrective actions in the process when necessary. Different perspectives and further options shall be reviewed by all parties involved preceding making further steps, according to adjustments made. Reaching key milestones, a reassessment of current positions, is an essential practice.

There is no dividing line between learning and doing. Any learning from mistakes, not only personal but also other's failures, can contribute to own effectiveness in operations. *Learning-by-doing* is an established concept in contemporary economic theory, by which productivity development is achieved through practice and adaptations. Learning through reflection of doing is beyond an intellectual exercise. It is based on contemplation of gained experience, tenancy in agreements, and readiness for adaptation of experience within ongoing engagement. The elements of each theory might be appropriate under distinction of the practical goals, depending on the circumstances. Chances of a durable competitive advantage are increasing with sincere quality approach and awareness of further contributions.

We live in an interconnected world—being rooted locally, yet, interacting globally. The continuous change has become endemic, as under the Web-incited dynamics, potential markets get beyond known boundaries of international rules and local regulations. Any local strategies for the definition of the sound planning toward execution of agreed actions shall be based on the understanding of the total goals and objectives. Conductive to address enhanced delivery obstacles, the transnational corporations need to reduce boundary limitations with attribution of own and partner capabilities. Very often, it is quite challenging to overcome obstacles. Strict focus on the ongoing efforts could be staggering. The challenge is in getting to the core of an issue through persistent review of the underlying causes and constructive probing of resulting effects.

Considering a posting in a foreign country, it is reasonable to identify and allocate a *coach* as a change agent with proven familiarity in the target cultural environment and also identify a mentor within the management team. With mutual acknowledgment of the shared topics, parties agree on the *modus operandi* and define goals, objectives, and strategies of collaboration that shall contribute to improved performance. While the coach is in charge of guiding the overall process and sessions, the ownership of the success criteria remains in personal merits. Adjacent to sessions, proposed exercises need to be performed to secure the desired effects. Mentorship is as well a reciprocal relationship. While the mentee gets advice for a new field of engagement, the mentor receives acknowledgment and can rely on receiving support in return. Certainly, local management can be open-minded to innovations. Following success in a subsidiary, it gets easier to scale results across the corporation. Communicating results from local projects at the group level, you can often benefit twofold—deploying contributions from the locally viable results by aiming at efficient and repeatable success across the organization.

In response to a perpetual renewal, there is a need for an adaptive transformation with meaningful measures of the achievements. Many times, *performance evaluation* has been backward-looking, while it can be more important to evaluate capabilities of the resources at hand for upcoming tasks. This is critical if one is about to initiate a new undertaking by the means of expanding business to new areas or ensure presence in developing markets. Within adaptation to new strategies, business managers better consider change mitigation within the roadmap on development efforts.

> It took me over three years to explore sound opportunities in a new country. Building on new contracts with international corporations for which we had to identify and enable local partners, we could recruit energetic and reliable staff. Most importantly, it took some time to establish cooperative relationships within vivid local networks that were influencing selection processes for new vendors. At the end, a solid business plan for a new financial year could be addressed in just half of the time. The executives of the company have been reassured about fair payback for the manageable investment. International partners could join and expand their business into further territories.

Over time, most things in the business environment change—some trends can be foreseen according to basic rules, several alterations are caused by circumstances, and few are truly disruptive. Each severe disruption could as well create numerous new opportunities for learning and growth. In the interest to seize it, it's worth unlocking for collaboration across different players in varied marketplaces. Investing efforts into mutually beneficial partnerships contributes to relevance within broader areas. While managers are primarily charged with building operationally efficient and self-sustaining structures, many changes occur driven by the external realities. Hence, internal structures ought to adapt to the complexities of the external conditions under which they operate.

Many of the multifarious phenomena remain valid despite novel alternatives in contextual perspectives across Western and Eastern business entities. Eastern management especially prefers to initiate one step after another rather than taking risks from disruptive jump leaps. By their measures, social impacts play just as important a role as economic aspects. You might notice, that within Eastern culture, "*small gifts maintain friendship*" and contribute to customer relationships. However, no one is obliged to this habit if it does not occur wholeheartedly. Paramount are structured (time-stamped) meeting minutes to capture content and decisions during business encounters. Upon formal exchange with counterparts, they can be reviewed and either confirmed or amended with their views. In any case, the efforts of taking and sharing meeting notes serve as a blueprint for further conduction of collaborative engagements.

As always, everyone needs to be flexible and adaptive to continuous changes in the marketplace. Increased pressures from accelerating technological advancement at all levels surely challenge constituents. Productivity improvement over time can be expected with continuous learning and experimentation. It is an effective method for leaders to embrace new initiatives and engage their subordinates toward any further opportunities, as discussed with certain propositions in the next chapter. Going forward, let's also review how communities of practice within company culture contribute to shaping the enterprise's ability for success.

Shen in the Sense of Community

True strength lies in the appropriate use of cause and effects. Added value can be created by reinforcing complementary goods. In any business relationship, there is a mix of technical, financial, and functional requirements that are often influenced by industrial trends, community regulations, and customer's needs. Agile leaders always encourage a systemic learning organization to achieve better teamwork, strategy, and process improvements. As influential actors, they can certainly interpret corporate policies as guidelines for implementation. This section

---

"*One of the most important keys to successful performance…is empowering everyone on the team to think and act like a leader.*" Alison Levine.

addresses suchlike and other related areas across the boundaries of societies.

Engaged in business transactions in a sense of shared destiny, communities can experience forces within and between their boundaries. One can benefit by creating long-lasting, trustworthy relationships. The ability to impart a vision statement, that addresses expectations of most stakeholders, is crucial. The quest is to gain a balance between dissimilar and unifying values in opposition to each other. The power of *TAO* acting as everlasting guidance is immanent within any realization (*TE*). Consider, how it can support you in extending the business objectives. Any broader goals can only be reached by the means of a fruitful cooperation. Such ingrained orchestration is free of determination thoughts—it assists in an integral development of achievements from the highest probability of possible actions. To get there, it is critical to make and articulate well-considered decisions that are based on practical measures. It can be assumed that strong leadership is based on oversight. Their colleagues and partners will be grateful for transparency.

We are increasingly confronted with combinations of globally scattered resources in diverse team structures. More often, projects are based on collaboration with social impact. Therefore, influential leaders propagate and advocate tolerance. Too much interference in the affairs of others, despite the best of personal intentions, can even lead to undesirable results. By looking at relational drives from several perspectives, we shall be able to explore how key performance indices could take disruptive tendencies into considerations and introduce measures for success in multidisciplinary projects that require cross-disciplinary knowledge, and metacognitive skills.

The disposition to think "*out of the box*" uncovers a wide range of possibilities. One should never underestimate people's ability to change. It's a pleasure to uncover true capabilities from self-regard and in relationship with others. The challenge lies in a pliable yet consistent behavior—flexibility makes new experience possible, while consistency provides a sense of reliability.

> One of my imperatives was to earn as much as possible on every business trip—perceived as a reward from being away from family and friends. Any possible tactic and technique would be used, from making *cold calls* at the trip destination to referential meetings to acquisition of partners to become multiplier of our offerings. Visiting a new place to sign off on a new stage in business development, ask your counterparts to get introduced to the local *power base* for the possibilities to uncover yet unexploited chances. The fee is just a bill for a dinner in a favorable location, the reward then follows as another opportunity for contractual closures, as illustrated below.

Any result-oriented actions must fit to personality. The deliberate posture needs to happen based on inner conviction and supported by outer conditions. Simply following one's inner beliefs in orientation to a single most obvious trend often leads to a tenuous position. A sensitive attention to all relevant affairs within the own areas across the spans of responsibility can expand to know when "*the time is ripe*" to perform. People must be clear about proper procedure or conduct for an activity. One of Warren Buffets verdicts is, "*risk comes from not knowing what you are doing.*"—especially with the lack of ability to foreseen economic implications of business decisions.

The corporate culture creates identity, but it can also become a limiting factor in a business model change. As such, it might be difficult to overcome a corporate immune system aware of core values. It may require external accelerators such as free market competition or strong opinions of key stakeholders to bring new perspectives to fruition. Some employees have the "talent" to leave a situation to the management of others. In fact, sometimes, it is better to avoid fierce competition that could lead to wasted investment. When you realize that the competitor is truly superior in certain situations, consider what else you can offer your target customers, or decide to focus on better ways to save valuable resources.

Most people appreciate social stability as a favorable environment for self-fulfillment. They look for a reciprocity in business relationships. Their focus on the common floor in terms of the group-dynamic in achieving common goals is expressed in the verse 9 of TTC

> *Fill your bowl to the brim and it will spill.*
> *Keep sharpening your knife and it will blunt.*
> *Chase after money and security and your heart will never unclench.*
> *Care about people's approval and you will be their prisoner.*
> *Do your work, then step back.*
> *The only path to serenity.*

Considering cyclical duality within natural processes, any enforced attempts to maximize ways and means constitute short-lived episodes, which are doomed to fail. Strategic alliances may range from a short-term engagement to address a particular opportunity, over coordinated efforts with complementary assets when entering an emerging market, to establishing a dominant platform over rivals.

In line with the realities of business prospects, it takes time and resources to build up values. As stated by Warren Buffett, "*no matter how great talent of effort, some things just take time.*" (Buffett and Clark 2008, p. 151) Often, only a retreat from a fierce competition can bring you forward. Only the more conscious robustness paired with vitality will prevail, as has been stated in the verse 69 of TTC

> *There is an old saying:*
> *"It is better to become the passive in order to see what will happen.*
> *It is better to retreat a foot than to advance only an inch."*
> *This is called being flexible while advancing,*
> *pushing back without using force,*
> *and destroying the enemy without engaging him.*
> *There is no greater disaster than underestimating your enemy.*
> *Underestimating your enemy means loosing your greatest assets.*
> *When equal forces meet in battle,*
> *victory will go to the one that enters with the greatest sorrow.*

With the rise of hybrid and distributed work models, *Gartner Group*[1] is predicting a mix of personal and professional goals, next to focus on team execution. Many successful leaders pay close attention to their practice benchmarking, which can be used as a comparison of key figures to gain better positions.

---

[1] gartner.com/en/articles/6-predictions-for-the-future-of-performance-management.

We can aim at achieving better results by thinking cyclically and globally, while acting locally. Broad goals and objectives are usually based on corporate vision and mission statements. They can be cascaded down via regional and country levels, with distinct planning of related actions. The GOSPA methodology[2] can get you there. Therein, distinct goals are expressed guideposts on the path to desired advancement, so that the related overarching quantifiable objectives can cover every aspect of business affairs. GOSPA driven hierarchical planning approach is fairly easy to appreciate and rather quick to implement. While realistic ***goals*** and clear ***objectives*** consider a long-term planning horizon, the sound ***strategies*** orient themselves at best advantages in the process of organizational development—the strategic orientation should strengthen existing potential and reduce critical dependencies. The derived execution ***plans*** then encompass certain ***actions*** aiming at securing important positions by responsible management—as exemplary illustrated in the following table, with the interlinked five areas covering major aspects of a sound plan.

Affirming common grounds, leaders bring cooperation to live. Their ability to create new chances through perceived difficulties can promote readiness for the resolution of hindering obstacles.

> With expansion into the new market, the board appointed a mature manager to set up the new department focusing on business development in the Eastern Europe. He tried to mirror his prior experience gained from roles in Canada and South Africa. A key challenge turned up in dealing with ongoing plagiarism. Under the copyright infringements, any further engagements were put in question. Yet, this way the company could not enter this market, realizing that it was not *business-as-usual*. There was a need to address differences in the light of new circumstances. For the beginning, there was a need to meet the trading challenge with adjusted purpose. Only with the mindset flexibility could another manager recognize new market potential and uncover ways of minimizing risks with the introduction of controlled dealership networks. His ability to construct specific realities and harness the uncertainty led to new practices for market development. His initial strategy went to consolidating

---

[2] An introduction is outlined on www.gospaplanning.com.

> a fragmented dealership through horizontal integration across the vast territory of the former Soviet Union. It allowed to implement tacit price coordination for our products. The empowered dealers have organized a promotion campaign and obeyed to agreed practices of joint offerings. Later one, having established a significant customer base, it was time to establish a wholly owned representative office by acquiring the most successful dealer and turning others to favorable partnership agreements in these promising markets.

GOSPA planning constitutes a vivid business model. As soon as new ideas have been set as *goals* and *objectives*, derived *strategies* and coordinated *plans* for the implementation of business processes with an extended radius of *actions* must follow. Own essential activities (*A*) are not freestanding but are linked with one another. They intrinsically relate to an execution plan (*P*) and reflect designed strategy (*S*) according to specific objectives (*O*) in line with the total goals (*G*) as expression of the desired outcome on the path of discovery.

Goal	Objective	Strategy	Plan	Actions		
				Who	When	Impact
Become a global player with innovative eBikes	Setup new line this year	Fit new chain rings	Setup team for new gear	COO	Early 2023	80 K €
		Retain spend expenditures	Define costs	CFO	Jan 2023	Set limits
			Consider rewards	HR	Feb 2023	10% in growth
	Enter Asian markets early next year	Synergy with new transport channel	New packaging	CPO	Q4 2023	5%
			Bulk shipment	COO	Q1 2024	60 K €
		Follow six sigma approach	Push through quality plan	CPO	M'ly	JIT process

In such an approach, one begins broadly in terms of a long-term vision, which is refined as each further definition of collective effort is made. Long-term *goals* are qualitative in nature. They get further advanced by quantifiable *objectives*. In turn, *strategies* aim at measurable results, so that related plans incorporate actions for realization. As such, every single goal as well as derived objectives and strategies must be not only interlinked, but also consistent with each other.

Companies must choose and decide on a right approach to pursue their objectives. There are manifold ways to the right mix of strategies that function together to achieve more with much less effort. It all stands and falls with the ability to mobilize resources around realistic plans, with capable management following through defined actions. As partly declared in the verse 1 of TTC, it functions along inseparable fundamental principles (*TAO*) and ongoing process (*TE*).

> *A way can be a guide, but not a fixed path;*
> *Names can be given, but permanent labels.*
> *Always passionless, thereby observe the subtle;*
> *ever intent, thereby observe the apparent.*
> *These two come from the same source but differ in name;*
> *both are considered mysteries.*

Goals and objectives shall be expressed in relation to what is happening. However, they become feasible only by the means of an expressed strategy initiating purposeful planning combining the most relevant actions. More often than expected, we get into uncharted waters, mostly trying to find the best-possible way forward. Therefore, better consider that only a follow-through execution links strategy with modes of operational planning.

There are several *functional leadership models*[3] that can be applied to the specification of business goals and objectives toward team cohesion. Their effectiveness relies on the organized flexibility and focuses on actions with periodic assessment of the performance. Only progressive leaders can motivate others in a way that is relevant to any skeptics who are seeking an inspiring sense of their engagement. By empowering fellow workers to make their own decisions and take appropriate actions, they can improve collective throughput. Such guidance has been stated in the verse 46 of TTC

---

[3] Most popular are discussed on totempool.com/blog/functional-leadership.

> *When the world has the Way,*
> *running horses are retired to till the fields.*
> *When the world lacks the Way,*
> *war-horses are bred in the countryside.*
> *No crime is greater than approving of greed;*
> *no calamity is greater than discontent,*
> *no fault is greater than possessiveness.*
> *So the satisfaction of contentment is always enough.*

The considerate management team is greater than its individuals when conflicts can be turned into creative forces. Attentive leaders retain a comprehensive overview and can calm down any concerns. They know how important it is to be content with what is going on than to get upset about missed chances. Not knowing how to get to a satisfactory solution and when to stop leads to double damage.

A flawless execution relies on an open communication of practical goals. If the balance is off within multi-perspective considerations across technological, financial, or social elements, there is a need to re-consider further aspects on the way to perceived development. Any substantial commitment for prosperity requires a cooperative, team building approach and appeal to a common purpose. On top of taking advantage of professional competence, a spirit aiming at reaching goals and objectives with desire to follow proposed strategy within defined planning of distinct actions would be a remarkable accomplishment for any manager. A free communication flow reduces confrontations and enables power workers for better results, driving further ingenuity from higher energy levels.

One does not have to accept a position of a formal "*Chief Communications Officer*" (CCO) to apply key requirements of such a position—possibly relying on the duties of public relations and affairs.

> One of my partners in business (he was a lawyer by education, and was partly serving duties as an investigator at Scotland Yard) pointed out, that if people are using plenty of words, they try to hide that they don't have much to say to the topic at hand.

Viable business decision-making takes place upon weighing evidence and examination of alternatives in advance of drawing conclusions for execution. Herewith, proven knowledge is equally important to thorough contemplation of concealed motifs.

Our "*gut feelings*" express personal awareness of hidden patterns in the surrounding world. They are always best to be considered—emotions are signals, especially, when forging a relationship. The odds are that under such critical circumstances, one might attain a rewarding outcome, while tough attempts to snatch a more advanced position are doomed to failure. Some character traits of a dependable leader that bolster an integrative worldview are particularly described in the verse 24 of TTC

> *One who boasts is not established;*
> *One who shows himself off does not become prominent;*
> *One who puts himself on display does not brightly shine;*
> *One who brags about himself gets no credit;*
> *One who praises himself does not long endure.*
> *In the Way, such things are called:*
> *"Surplus food and redundant action."*
> *And with things – there are those who hate them.*
> *Therefore, the one with the Way in them does not dwell.*

We cannot neglect opposing tendencies in our surroundings. Resolution of unnatural traits implies a reconceptualization of leadership. Forged trials in taking any credit for other's achievements to snatch a more advanced position are not lasting. Striving leaders avoid overdone conduct as an excessive blemish.

An illustrative role-model in relation to a *mission statement* could as well be a *performance benchmark* to aim for. In doing so, the outliers shall be reconsidered and further adjusted to reach a coherent scheme of the aligned objectives toward encompassing goals. Situational awareness, when paired with capability analysis, leads to a foundation for the balanced action planning. A sound strategy would further evolve as circumstances change.

Cross-cultural leadership is not flaunting by virtue of positional placement. Especially during times of turbulent changes, the adoption rate to realities in the dynamics of emerging markets can suffer. A useful practice can be a regular discussion with peers in foreign countries on how their business might change in a year from now. Only fair partnership can form lasting business associations. Taking into considerations that each company has the own agenda, a joint business planning can capture shared cascading objectives and define agreed strategies for execution. Different aspects can be reviewed to judge on the probability of the unruly conditions. Conductive to specific business objectives, leaders prefer to establish collaborative and participative partnership. Success across, a globally operating consultancy for diversity management and cross-cultural competence development, states in its News-Story 8/2012[4] *"One way to approach an efficient and trustful partnership is the development of a "third culture." In workshops, the "new" coworkers define values and rules on how one wishes to work together. This circumvents political power games and the frictional loss that comes with pushing through the one or the other corporate culture."*

Coaching is important in successful manager's portfolio[5] aiming at full potential of their staff. It encourages a learning environment that ensures continuous development from probing questions and constructive feedback. Every individual has strengths, weaknesses, opportunities, and threats. An experienced coach does not try to change their essence but rather supports the individuals in realizing their distinct qualities that can be applied toward achieving common goals. Applying the coach-and-support leadership style, she is keen on passing valuable insights to peers and subordinates, expanding collectively available capabilities of their organization.

With assumed liability, one also needs to care for rewarding relationships in respect to the common saying, and *"a team is only as good as its leader."* Continuous observation of *group dynamics* occurring in work processes is a source of compelling direction, supportive context, and enabling attitude. It is fair to restate given assignments based on changed conditions. Ability for a multifactorial analysis of market attractiveness and business strengths can help to avoid unexpected affairs. Be prepared to consider valid adjustments to intended strategy as a result of changing

---

[4] See successacross.com/en/publications.
[5] See en.wikipedia.org/wiki/Coaching#Business_and_executive.

reality. Don't be afraid to reset the course of actions, as far as they stay in line with the overall objectives.

According to the growth mindset, any process adjustments and iterations in planning shall only be considered in line with the expectations of key stakeholders. Rewards are due to happen if we assess the risks and challenges right. It's fair to be pleased by reaching targets, and unbiased motivation will remain at a higher level upon achievement of intermediate goals. As to how to address goals and meet objectives in a balanced manner with short- and long-term considerations, several dimensions, such as profitability, innovation, market coverage, and customer and employee satisfaction, must be covered. When developing novel and innovative business processes and revenue streams, the *customer value maximization* (CVM) framework[6] could become a reasonable value driver.

Ongoing mapping of current positions in the views of customers' trends and competitive offerings shall be done against interactions within the target markets. Each targeted customer and every market segment require a dedicated plan with outlined best- vs. worst-case scenarios for discussion with peers for the assessment of the needed efforts, known risks and potential rewards.

Deng Xiaoping has been the paramount leader in the transformation of the People's Republic of China, standing on equal terms with global powers. He had carried out the pragmatic course of *"The Four Modernizations"* with the aim of increasing economic efficiency through reforms—incl. opening of the enterprises, flexibility in the use of labor and inflow of foreign capital. The changes were preferably made in stages to protect the participants in these processes from being overwhelmed. In particular, the migrant workers enable the emergence of profitable commercial companies. Their contribution has secured modernization of many industrial branches. Since then, the Chinese society is moving with far-reaching mobility toward classless structures. The Chinese government carefully tries to spread proven principles of change, like cascades between different heights in a chalky formation of mountain range.

---

[6] See en.wikipedia.org/wiki/Customer_value_maximization.

Successful entrepreneurs there implement David Ricardo's theory of *comparative advantage*.

A regular strategy review can reveal valuable potential to leverage the scale of the future business scope upon profitable growth from the core. The verse 33 in TTC is broadly arguing about attributions of inner resources toward strengths of accomplished self-mastery.

> *He, who knows others is wise;*
> *he who knows himself is enlightened.*
> *He who conquers others has physical strength.*
> *He who conquers himself is strong.*
> *He who is contended is rich.*
> *He who acts with vigour has will.*
> *He who does not lose his place will endure.*
> *He who dies but does not really perish enjoys long life.*

Credible leaders share their values and convictions and demonstrate consistency between their beliefs and actions. The *authentic leader* combines self-awareness, responsiveness to feedback, and conflict resolution competency in non-manipulative ways with lasting potential. Clear intentions and prosperity targets can only be achieved when being in peace with oneself.

Experienced managers are considerate in choosing appropriate incentives and encourage their subordinates to go the extra mile. Motivational incentives can be an integral part of corporate culture. All rewards must be relevant to achievements that encourage specific expected contributions. My experience is that empowerment pays off sooner rather than later.

While employees in mature markets appreciate the flexibility in working conditions or participation in stock options programs, the personnel in developing countries often prefer additional rewards as direct financial allowances (i.e., in Russia), or as a career aspiration (e.g., in India).

The largest software company in Germany is known for its generous incentive programs that increase employees' loyalty to the corporation. The

> new manager of its car fleet department has initiated an expansion of the mobility policy. Under new conditions, an eligible employee in Germany can now decide to get instead of a gas, electric, or plug-in car also an annual railway ticket. Each employee can as well lease an eBike and take it over after two years of usage – that has been implemented at other companies across Germany as well.

In the modern world, social development is affected with the massive and rapid flow of information. Agile organizations can learn to move business value from customer insights into adaptation of products and services. Ahead of initiating the next phase in the everlasting cycles, inspiring leader needs to recap points of engagement.

> One of my supervisors was gifted in articulating purposeful questions. At the end of each business day, he would recapitulate results in relation to our priorities. It supported reflection on the achieved contributions to the core objectives. We knew that he was sincerely interested in constructive feedback. This way we could get aligned on the next stages in development.

To be on the safe side, it helps to have a mental compass that aligns the required execution with company policies. At the bottom line, though, it is about respect of the attention we borrow from our counterparts in any meeting. They need to agree to your views on the situation, proposed actions and expected results. Even previously uncovered inconsistencies could contribute to further insights and trigger new ideas—the yield is a shared vision, as in the verse 40 of TTC

> *Return is the movement of the Tao.*
> *Yielding is the way of the Tao.*
> *All things are born of being.*
> *Being is born of non-being.*

The reverse interplay of fundamental principles and natural processes is never ending. Avoidance of insincere interactions can be conductive to social harmony. By reaching one extreme, a reversal process takes place.

Only authentic communication can persuade the audience. Emotionally arousing declarations describing appealing scenarios surely make a stronger impression than animated pictures in a slide deck. Cyclical creation and expiration depend on each other, flawless practice discloses mastering, any commitment or refusal best appear in light of alternatives.

There are considerations for a business presentation to convey important information to a group of professionals or decision makers. When in front of an audience, the ability to storytelling by using common artifacts and symbolic means can be quite helpful. Slide shows are one-way illustrations of a proposition that has been prepared offline. They are less effective than an online expression of a given situation. Rather than using a slide deck prepared in advance, the *WYSIWIG* notion unfolds best by drawing key elements by stating relevant components of the matter at hand on a flip chart or white board.[7] If you can interactively unfold the storyline in front of the audience, they see you working to address a particular issue at hand.

An authentic content shall emerge in front of the audience so that they can make up their mind about expressed genuine messages. Ideally, supported by a discussion with the participants, you could present viable options toward an expected solution. This way you could mix objective facts with personal views in a reflection of arguments within a shared context. Done well, it sparks an atmosphere of collaboration. Exchange of arguments is a combination of proven facts, implicit assumptions, persistent perceptions, and common views under given circumstances.

> Invited as a keynote speaker at an international conference (in St. Petersburg) I've prepared an illustrative slide deck as it was a common practice in those days. However, during the flight, my laptop ran out of power and no one at the errand had a fitting power supply at hand. Fortunately, the storyline was available as a printout, so that key messages could be verbally articulated to the audience, although without supporting images. It had ripple effect for following fruitful discussions. This experience has clearly shown that trying to enlist others in your pitch, you can avoid sophisticated slides in a presentation format. A

---

[7] Useful tips are provided by Garr Reynolds on www.presentationzen.com

> solid structure in conveying key messages, avoiding non-essential matters and demonstrating way out of illustrated issues lingers longer with the audience.

Our social identity arises from the joined efforts and shared achievements of a purposeful community we have selected to join. The ability to overcome social imprint can be a plus. Within a defragmented matrix organization, employees at many levels are posed to make trade-offs in working relationships. Continuously, Sun Tzu's "Art of War," influenced by classical Taoism, is consulted for leadership advice. It teaches us, among others, that an overall strategy is inert without adjusted behaviors. My supervisor has ordered copies of this book for distribution across his regional management group. We could use it as a reference when discussing target account strategy to generate resourceful growth plan.

A business culture characterized by humility and restraint can produce uncovered qualities. Consistent quality in customer service pays off in multiple ways. It pays to inspire people to take responsibility and unleash their potential within the framework of company goals. Completion of an important undertaking provides a sense of excitement. It's worth being properly celebrated with those who made significant contributions to success.

Large-scale projects with customers that operate globally shall never be impaired by the own organizational boundaries. Such engagements always require appropriate due diligence and planning, and rigorous built-in change control processes. A vital task of a seasoned leader is the development of sustainable policy competence.

> I was fortunate to get invited several times to the "President's Club" events. On top of a pleasant experience of visiting great locations, the most rewarding are intensive contacts with executives from different parts of the organization and geographies. The chance to work with great leaders and take up on their proven techniques is surely the best way of creating networks aiming at a better workplace. The European president – later in charge of EMEA and APJ regions – had an extraordinary ability to articulate unique value propositions for company offerings lasting over

> coming years. Depending on any further disruptions, we applied specific market conditions to them.

In the commitment to the course taken, successes are usually attributed to reliable partnerships. We need to look for partners who can support or complement our services. Working together to achieve common goals increases *steward leadership*. The ability to use one's own company's capabilities effectively to achieve the best-possible solution to common goals cannot be taken for granted. By cooperating in corporate networks, a *thought leader* achieves a wider reach of influence through regular (or even random) visits to partner companies. Such fruitful collaboration can refresh situational awareness and revitalize connections within enduring collaborative networks.

Nowadays, most enterprises operate in a more complex and competitive environment than ever. Given permanent changes in the flowing state, size does not really matter. It is practically impossible to overlook innumerable interactions in business conduct. A leader is characterized by being able to see complex issues in context. Hybrid work methods with structural alterations can trigger several consequences, such as increased requirements on security and detachment from peers. The verse 73 of TTC is pointing to natural positions of broader cooperation within mutual dependencies

> *If you're brave in being daring, you'll be killed;*
> *If you're brave in not being daring, you'll live.*
> *With these two things,*
> *in one case there's profit, in the other there's harm.*
> *The things Heaven hates – who knows why?*
> *The Way of Heaven is not to fight yet to be good at winning,*
> *not to speak yet skilfully respond.*
> *– No one summons it, yet it comes on its own –*
> *To be at ease yet carefully plan. Heaven's net is large and vast;*
> *Its mesh may be coarse yet nothing slips through.*

The clear advice here is to refrain from unnecessary interventions, as strengths comes from flexibility, and courage is most effective only when it gets tempered by gentle prudence.

Global businesses are exposed to further insecurities, from an increased level of complexity and uncertainty. Getting to the tipping point, better results can be reached with a supportive attitude. We need to act in a constraint environment, yet our responsibility can strengthen social cohesion.

One surely needs to consider changing market conditions that may severely impact the company's performance. A deliberate introduction of a change could be triggered by a compelling event. It can be challenging to deploy certain events and seize the potential of a tipping point within the mainstream of regular business development.

Many verses in TTC affirm the necessity of managed cooperation. A key point from this chapter is that in favor of cooperation for mutual benefits, the Taoist view turns "*I*" to "*We*" that is based on trust as the central quality in human relationships. Only the members of a well-managed team perform at their best.

> My latest manager grew into a role model of exemplary leaders by being able to align actions with shared fate. Considering the needs and interests of team members, he made it a rule to share all information at his hands for successful development of the alignment processes. Every team member and his close confidants were kept up to date on relevant business strategies. He was able to constantly go about encouraging initiatives in others and building faithful employees within a strong teamwork.

> Applying thorough listening skills, he could be aligned on perspectives, jointly aiming at extraordinary results. In communicating his beliefs, he ensured that his direct reports and peers could better understand the reasoning behind certain recommendations for actions.

> Conduction of regular team calls has contributed to renewed commitment based on the common set of principles. In a spirit of high standard of

> performance with an attempt to address new challenges, every teammate could inquire on status and ask for help along the way. Ongoing one-to-one conversations have always supported the individual's growth. The affirmation of shared values allowed for the acceptation notion of special significance for our contributions. At the bottom line, it was rewarding to realize that our contributions got noticed by management and been recognized across business lines.

It's time to see how Taoism is transforming through globalization.

Héxié Within Globalization

Global advancements in business are usually seen as inevitable. *Globalization*, though, can be a double-edged sword. It promotes the introduction of compatible standards—from creation of balance sheets to the use of charging cables for mobile devices. Steadily, it became a new norm requiring constant adaptation to recurring changes in the distribution of resources, constantly driven by the introduction of new technologies and work processes. Any reasonable considerations in overcoming restraints in a multitude of areas demand appreciation of an

---

"*The secret of success is to do the common thing uncommonly well.*" John D. Rockefeller Jr.

overarching *ecosystem*. Progress sometimes follows contradictory trends in international relations, so that overdrawn efforts can reach beyond the *economic equilibrium*. Let's try to commence this section with the view on the multiple opportunities for international enterprises in the global marketplace.

The globalization of the economy has introduced a host of factors that are leading to frequent reorganizations. The times for cheap offshoring of Western technologies to China or Southeast Asia are over. There are no more undeveloped low-cost regions with the necessary capacities there either. No matter how convoluted the own business model is, it can only sustain in a dynamic balance with the influencing powers (*TAO*) by taking into consideration broader temporal and spatial ranges of dynamic adjustments (*TE*).

In dealing with China or SE Asia, we shall consider prevailing structural conditions. Next to the expertise of the own business, it requires an extensive attention to variations in the conditions.

Thus, let's review how *TAO* "*imbues all things, including global trade and mobility*" throughout the world[1] within complex value chains. The *Taoist leader* can at once seize multiple perspectives and seek consensus in decision-making by marking business integrity with social responsibility.

Even in the current era of *post-globalization* toward a less connected world, an expansion from matured countries into the emerging markets will continue. National states are now striving for greater economic independence, although liberalized free trade and the division of labor continue to make an important contribution to general prosperity. The risks to be assessed lay in the process, i.e., dealing with fewer reliable partners for supply chains. Due to the new geopolitics, it can be necessary to look for further business partners and consider alternative delivery routes to improve logistical efforts. When dealing with complexity and embracing interdependencies, we could try out convergence of harmonious leadership.

Taking to excess any of the outstanding strengths can be counterproductive. Suitable collaboration in social networks really matters. Connecting the right people for the envisioned journey leads to a

---

[1] See www.worldwideerc.org/news/mobility/the-tao-of-globalization

rewarding experience. Reasonable usage of material and capital resources is displayed in the verse 53 of TTC

> *If I understood only one thing,*
> *I would want to use it to follow the Tao.*
> *My only fear would be one of pride.*
> *The Tao goes in the level places,*
> *but people prefer to take the short cuts.*
> *If too much time is spent cleaning the house*
> *the land will become neglected and full of weeds,*
> *and the granaries will soon become empty*
> *because there is no one out working the fields.*
> *To wear fancy clothes and ornaments,*
> *to have your fill of food and drink*
> *and to waste all of your money buying possessions*
> *is called the crime of excess.*
> *Oh, how these things go against the way of the Tao!*

Taoism highlights the concept of conscious *harmony* with natural laws as an ongoing process of creation and preservation. Harmony exists when dynamics in the relationships of related components can develop without significant resistance. It is best to build up entrepreneurial ability for organizational recovery ahead of any upcoming business crisis. The observation "*never let a good crisis go to waste*" is attributed to Sir Winston Churchill. Autonomy in action when driving success home in a self-reflection of personal agenda by balancing everything has been pointed up in the verse 77 of TTC

> *The Way of heaven is like drawing a bow:*
> *the high is lowered, the low is raised;*
> *excess is reduced, need is fulfilled.*
> *The Way of heaven reduces excess and fills need,*
> *but the way of humans is not so:*
> *they strip the needy to serve those who have too much.*

It's advisable to take preventive measures to secure own business, executing a practice of leveling up extreme tasks with the focus on the sustainable business growth. Fair distribution of income among stakeholders leads to investment portfolio amelioration. Such a corrective attitude supports the way of though in *being* responsive for a long-term success rather than its compensation in *doing* impermanent positions toward volatile gains. Based on regular compensation benchmarking, equitable distribution of income can ensure fairness and allow everyone to participate in the upcoming opportunities.

Although, globalization is a pervasively unsettling process, we certainly gain maturity from an understanding of broader connotations. We are in a constant process, characterized by changes and continuity, which is occasionally accompanied by upheavals. We should understand characteristic behaviors to arrive at differentiated patterns of success. In line with the practice of social modernization in Asian countries, the "*power base*" supporting leaders in Central and SE Asia can be best understood in terms of networks. There are certain grids of mentorship established along the personal career path, crisscross of support connecting corporations to financial services via the bond market and other strong relationships down to reciprocal commitments within a clan affiliation.

We can streamline energy flow to reach desired state only with focus on essential factors. It is much better to put own energy into a durable competitive advantage of an exceptional corporation. Any of the transnational product strategies shall consider localization efforts within economies of scale. Commonly, only success at strategic accounts can make or break desirable target achievement. For that matter, the underlying meaning of "*strategic*" primarily implies importance to the business of a distinct enterprise. Multinational companies better have ways of frequent exchange of experience by bringing representatives from subsidiaries abroad together for exchange. They could bring new ideas to be considered as valuable initiatives worth distribution across geographies. Such cross-border activities can contribute to overall cost savings, thus reducing expenditures for considered expansion strategies. We shall honor the bold move of Rob McEwen as Goldcorp's CEO in 2000 as he launched the so-called "*Goldcorp Challenge*."

> The Goldcorp challenge was about sharing the corporation's geological data (considered as a key asset in mining companies) with the public, asking for its analysis and offering a significant prize for best results. It has

> led to a wealth of new ideas that could dramatically shorten exploration time frames. The courage to take risks helped turn the company from a struggling enterprise into one of the most profitable in the mining industry.

As an acknowledged expert in geopolitics, Parag Khanna has recently pointed out in "The Future is Asian: *Global Order in the 21st Century*" that Asia accounts for 2/3 of the global growth. Writing about conducting commerce there, he has been predicting that the new Asian multicultural order will rather sooner than later result in greater coherence across the *Four Asian Tigers*. They benefit from forms of government that strengthen a leadership's ability to ensure sustained economic growth. Striving for local profit is viewed as an instrument for global success. Coordination between the decentralized branches of a company should contribute to the best-possible consensus.

International cooperation benefits from the ability to "*think globally.*" Far-sighted leaders have always been critical of the phenomenon of global labor arbitrage. They perceive the employees as a "*core asset.*" Which other market forces affect the development of companies? A true holistic vision can only come from intercultural experience. It leads to a better understanding of the own strengths and an open mind to suggestions for unorthodox solutions.

Most leadership skills have universal application. A steward leader can use underlying "forces" to get determined actions done through others. The cornerstone of any process is people being either involved therein or posed throughout its execution. It requires distinct skills to turn a company around when it gets into trouble—business as usual would only contribute to misery. Unbiased acknowledgment of various points of view with understanding of the patterns helps, as stated in the verse 22 of TTC

> *If you want to become whole, first let yourself become broken.*
> *If you want to become straight, first let yourself become twisted.*
> *If you want to become full, first let yourself become empty.*
> *If you want to become new, first let yourself become old.*
> *Those whose desires are few gets them,*

> *those whose desires are great go astray.*
> *For this reason the Master embraces the Tao,*
> *as an example for the world to follow.*
> *Because she isn't self centred, people can see the light in her.*
> *Because she does not boast of herself, she becomes a shining example.*
> *Because she does not glorify herself, she becomes a person of merit.*
> *Because she wants nothing from the world,*
> *the world cannot overcome her.*
> *When the ancient Masters said, "If you want to become whole,*
> *then first let yourself be broken," they weren't using empty words.*
> *All who do this will be made complete.*

Chinese managers are more likely to practice paradoxical leadership. The above statements point to the unity of opposites and provide an insight into the dynamics of development by using paradoxes, in a way that fragments build a whole, even when they at first hide the intermediate results in the completed form. You can even overcome obstacles ahead of gaining acceptance of being correct. Full spectrum of unbiased solutions requires a thorough selection process, so that consequently any improved capacity utilization grows best from tested and proven capabilities.

Globalization has led to an increase in trade enabled by international capital with the spread of products, technology, information, and jobs across national borders. An early entry into new markets can still be developed into a staying presence—the prudent traveler prepares well before the journey. Curiosity and pioneering spirit can be useful in the anticipation of expectations specific to the target markets. Only awareness of key trends in that industry and their benchmark position against peers will open doors for sensitive discussions. The profound understanding of customers purchasing patterns will provide crucial perception of the investment trends of a particular industry.

Navigating global markets means balancing international resources and capabilities with customization to local customer needs under constraints of regulations. Herewith, it pays off to follow recommendations of local staff on established habits. In Eastern Europe, it is important to bring a symbolic gift for the personal assistant of the executive board. At business meetings in China, even the choice of cigarettes, you bring can play a role—from the Zhonghua brand in red pack when establishing relationships to the prominent Panda brand from Shanghai in celebrating successful deal closing.

Globalization has also meant that the counterparties can adjust to largely the same conditions for entrepreneurial success across national borders. Supported by globally active financial institutions and ever-expanding logistics chains, a wide variety of value chains have emerged. Enterprises have increasingly adapted to the *just-in-time manufacturing* requirements. Know-how and technological advances become globally interconnected. Trends that are initiated in one part of the business world can expand into other industries and spread to other geographies. It would go far beyond the scope of this treatise if we went into the specifics of industries herein—each has special dynamics that you better learn to understand and consider. It can be observed that the advancements of technological evolution outperform linear progression. Their flexible transition encourages bold moves paired with adaptability to changing market conditions.

Everyone surely wants to avoid getting caught up in unbalanced affairs that limit effectiveness. There are increasing tensions between advanced economies and emerging markets. Any effort to resolve any inevitable conflicts between prevailing globalization and increasing localization comes with enormous challenges. Modern societies increasingly resist sacrificing their distinct cultural and organizational strengths in favor of sharing in the benefits of modernization. Taoism encourages collaboration by adopting different perspectives from an exchange of positions. The balanced mixture of empathy and activity leads to solidarity in the joint effort. Such an idea of optimizing available resources requires self-cultivation in many ways, next to a deep understanding of the basic concepts in business processes.

The call is with (informed) decision-making for fewer hierarchies in simplified structures. Upon clearly outlined assumptions and insights from practice, a networking team can assess diverse perspectives into genuine values for viable solutions, as it has been provocatively described in the verse 19 of TTC

> *Forget about knowledge and wisdom,*
> *and people will be a hundred times better off.*

> *Throw away charity and righteousness,*
> *and people will return to brotherly love.*
> *Throw away profit and greed, and there won't be any thieves.*
> *These three are superficial and aren't enough*
> *to keep us at the centre of the circle, so we must also:*
> *Embrace simplicity. Put others first. Desire little.*

These whimsical suggestions on how to bring people back to naturalness, simplicity, and genuineness aim to re-discover the benefits of simplicity. Taoism prefers a "*pure and unadorned*" state of being to retain holistic status, free from external objects. The Chinese logogram for purity *su* 素 originally means "*undyed raw silk.*" In the long term, any success is determined from authentic handling of these properties as "*an unimpaired spirit.*"

With globalization contributing to equality of market mechanisms, there is growth of middle class in current Greater China as well as in developing countries. In effect, China does not conform any longer to the pattern of a single state. It rather consists of several unique and rather powerful regions, such as Shanghai or Guangzhou metropolitan areas, or Dalian in Liaoning province. Currently, in China, there is an increase in market price with the rising labor costs at a surcharge of 10% and more, also due to better annual wages and salaries as an important factor. Considered profit margins can decrease accordingly for better education leading to critical thinking and self-expression. Following accession to *The World Trade Organization* (WTO), many corporations there faced the need to reform the employment relations. Chinese governance has undertaken pragmatic adaptation of the administrative accountability. It is perceived as a way of simplifying the contractual framework in par with reducing the administrative burden, toward enhanced transparency. Albeit significant progress made over past years, its truthful efficiency still needs to be further improved, technically contrary to the increasing tendency to incremental experimentation. The implications may be subtle, but still important for collaborative undertakings.

It is by no means trivial to survey the effects of *deregulation*—as it is being promoted in the telecommunications or energy industries within matured markets, for example. During the implementation, new forms of organization emerge and the most agile makers can step forward. This provides excellent opportunities to forge closer relationships with market leaders from abroad. On top, deregulation in the developing markets offers enormous opportunities for their connection to the world markets. Exaggerated expectations can lead to wrong decisions. It pays off to know how an upcoming disorder can be avoided. Within agile organizations, employees shall be empowered to contribute to changes. We experience *millennials* moving further toward *on-demand* business models and *sharing economy* with availability of goods or services for defined periods of time. Such transition leads to an ongoing transformation of internal processes.

Clearly, the rigid *hire and fire* mentality does not support moral of the employees, and it does not mean that toward securing natural harmony in stability one cannot release employees who do not follow the company's vision and mission objectives. In an intuitive process of discovery and exploration, the *vision statement* should be owned by all stakeholders. The increase in complex processes is a blocking factor to agile development. Even a gifted leader must take existing hierarchies and functioning networks into account—just think of the many efforts of Julius Caesar on his road to success.

Globalization has intensified worldwide cooperation. It now offers a wide range of meaningful formations but can also have controversial facets. Efforts to lower production costs and increase sales by opening up new markets are two sides of this coin. Improved efficiencies from formal performance management and monitoring efforts may slightly contribute to expected profit drivers. One should not underestimate the importance of social relationships between partner firms, with the comprehension of how credible commitment relies on feedback procedures. The known saying from Lenin "*trust is good, control is better*" has retained its meaning chiefly for alliance management. Implementation of partnerships with foreign suppliers in a network structure contributes to cost containment measures.

The most successful enterprises, like SAP, prevail in the execution of dual manner in the cooperative relationship with key players in the markets. Microsoft, for instance, could be seen on one side as an opponent for *Business Intelligence*, but on the other side as a strategic partner that is offering Cloud computing platform *Azure*. Siemens is a development partner on *Cloud for Energy*, but competes with SAP on the solutions for the *Internet of things*. IBM can be supportive of the *Hybrid Cloud* initiative while competing in services and so on.

Multinational corporations should be able to simultaneously seek strategic alignment across its network of business units. Among their essential considerations are the creation of additional value from global scale and scope efficiencies. For many ventures, it is a paradigm shift to address severe regional challenges with aligned enterprise-wide objectives. It requires an overall framework (i.e., by the means of a *balanced scorecard*[2] approach) and application of good *governance* to gage *regulatory compliance* while in transition. To be aware of what can hinder the dynamic nature of target objectives surely helps.

Willingness to an open conversation is decisive for success in any wide-ranging engagements. One can encourage realistic expectations by showing appreciation for significant contributions of teammates. Harmony in business ventures leads to improved group efforts, as outlined in the case study "Spiritual Wisdom of Taoism in Business" depicted at Cisco.[3] It helps to bring own expectations in unison with the given circumstances so that one can positively achieve the best-possible outcome.

> Some software companies are investing into industrial solutions, driven by the strategy shift that future revenue growth would depend on targeted applications of leapfrog technology to justify premium pricing. Having worked successfully with railways, we could also participate in an extraordinary European railroad's executive meeting. After attending a half-day of overview sessions to picture the most critical areas for improvements, there was a unique setting of one-to-one meetings with the representatives of each rail company present at this event—ranging from France, Germany, Switzerland to the Baltic States and CEE countries. In an open atmosphere, we got a chance to discuss their business issues and our capabilities of offerings to align on the scope of mutually beneficial projects.

---

[2] See en.wikipedia.org/wiki/Balanced_scorecard.
[3] Described in eprints.qut.edu.au/67646/1/67646.pdf.

> This was a most effective way to get access to extraordinary business insights and match them with our abilities for considerable improvements.

Some of the emerging markets experience fragile conditions. Yet, any intention of dominance could offend locals there. An offensive confrontation gets you into combat zones sooner rather than later. The verse 68 of TTC outlines the "*virtue of non-competition*" of the skillful leaders that retain their subjectivity at all levels by stating

> *The best warriors do not use violence.*
> *The best generals do not destroy indiscriminately.*
> *The best tacticians try to avoid confrontation.*
> *The best leaders becomes servants of their people.*
> *This is called the virtue of non-competition.*
> *This is called the power to manage others.*
> *This is called attaining harmony with the heavens.*

Contextual aspects play a contingent role for business risk mitigation and conflict prevention. Rather than enforcing dominance, inciting unreasoning errors from opponents could lead to better results. Leading managers do not try to attain excellent performance simply by establishing constraints and limitations. They rather turn legitimate measures into account to nurture creativity of cross-border specialists and coordinate efforts across disparate entities.

Benevolent ruling lies in aspiring to a state of natural grounds of sincere participation. Endeavors of a harmony with the natural conditions and social orders are expressed in the verse 65 of TTC

> *The ancient Masters who understood the way of the Tao,*
> *did not educate people, but made them forget.*
> *Smart people are difficult to guide,*
> *because they think they are too clever.*
> *To use cleverness to rule a country, is to lead the country to ruin.*
> *To avoid cleverness in ruling a country,*
> *is to lead the country to prosperity.*
> *Knowing the two alternatives is a pattern.*
> *Remaining aware of the pattern is a virtue.*
> *This dark and mysterious virtue is profound.*

It is opposite our natural inclination,
but leads to harmony with the heavens.

All these statements require a state of receptive mind unconstrained by biased judgments in valuing distraction. Experienced managers refrain from preventing their subordinates from using their candid knowledge, which could be applied to benefit of the overall goals.

Strategic thinking mindset proves its worth, especially under complex conditions. Strategy development interrelates with the introduction of balanced scorecards. Each scorecard supports repositioning toward achievement of goals and objectives matching measurable progress of defined key *performance indicators* covering *financial* controls, proper responsiveness to key *customer* demands, proven human capital management within *internal business processes*, and strengthened by innovative development via *learning and growth*.

> When the Russian financial markets experienced a great recession, SAS Institute decided to keep its local staff in Moscow onboard, using some of them for the expansion into Central Asia. The long-term strategy has proven that if you expect your business to grow, it pays to establish stakeholders and stay as close as possible to the customer. In particular, the president of a leading universal insurance companies there became keen on the Balanced scorecard (BSC) approach to align their business activities to the improved vision of the expanding organization. He used our consultancy to define and balance targets related to key financial, customer, staff and productivity goals confirmed by the board of directors.

The willingness to benefit others will always get appreciated. There are certain ways of non-intervening management of unbiased leaders leading to expected outcome as summarized in the verse 66 of TTC

The reason why rivers and seas can be lords of the hundred valleys
is that they lower themselves to them well;
therefore they can be lords of the hundred valleys.
So when sages wish to rise above people,
they lower themselves to them in their speech.
When they want to precede people, they go after them in status.
So when sages rule, people don't take it gravely.

*And when sages are in the forefront, people don't attack them.
Because they do not contend,
no one in the world can contend with them.*

Driven by the desire to diminish burdens, a responsible leader puts personal interests aside in closing the gap for a common good. Waterways and the sages can act effectively because they use accommodation rather than coercion in dealing with their environment.

Nowadays, enterprises must grow into agile structures from the attention on adaptation of best practices and with flexibility of self-organization in the business cycles. Ability for stimulated adoption of best practices will surely help to gain better results. Profound skills are rooted in the genuine understanding of recognizable patterns. The *knowledge sharing* processes are encompassing *best practices* and *good governance* policies that represent how an extraordinary content can be generalized, validated, and distributed across the international organization. Well-structured knowledge transfer has a direct impact on the efficiency of sales and delivery arrangements.

> At SAS Institute, we have successfully introduced the *knowledge management* system across the international Services organization, mainly with the aim to obtain *repeatable efficient success*. Participating consultants with the pre-sales or delivery focus, as well as project managers, have been rewarded with formal acknowledgement or even bonuses for their contributions to a centralized structured pool including the project documentation and code samples. A mandatory yet flexible review process was avoiding rigid structures while insuring extant relevance to corporate objectives.

When developing global markets and deploying economies of scope, a team approach is enclosing several business units. The organizational structure shall support regional proximity, reinforcing both employee and customer intimacy. Many conditions we take for granted can be in flux for significant periods of time. Off-times a severe recession is taking tall on business and governments that in consequence try to take on new roles in national economies. In critical situations, we need to discover fundamental principles of development and nurture vital ingredients for growth. Acting president of *Sun Microsystems*, Jonathan Schwarz, has stated that in the twenty-first century, "*we're entering an era in which people are participating rather than just receiving information.*"

The *financial services* sector appreciates proven solutions that could be seamless deployed across borders. Within international expansion, sound contributions of best practices get recognized and appreciated. Howbeit, certain local regulations require adjustments to worked out solutions, as well as licensing arrangements.

> Leading software companies put significant efforts into the creation of the Banking Industry Solutions as an integrated framework combining logical business models with underlying physical data representation at visualization layers. Upon selling such a package to a growing commercial bank in Ukraine aiming to comply with the international standards, we conducted a thorough investigation into a so-called "fit/gap analysis". It turned out that certain regulations issued by the local National Bank as well as mission-critical legacy systems required an adaptation. With the agreement on a multi-year contract, we could mobilize international experts leading growing numbers of local resources for agile implementation striving to the acceptable returns. Major benefits incl. integration across lines of business and simplified maintenance. We gained market know-how from this engagement and came up with a viable solution package to suit growing needs in this area.

When doing business abroad, one might face some paradoxes that at first sight might appear absurd but bear an appropriate meaning underneath. Most behaviors comprise their opposites. We might need certain stability to master change, the ability to balance of success and failure, and global regulations when empowering regional representations—as it has been expressed in the verse 36 of TTC

> *If you want to shrink something, you must first allow it to expand.*
> *If you want to get rid of something, you must first allow it to flourish.*
> *If you want to take something, you must first allow it to be given.*
> *This is called the subtle perception of the way things are.*
> *The soft overcomes the hard. The slow overcomes the fast.*
> *Let your workings remain a mystery.*
> *Just show people the results.*

We are now assuming that the central banks will be able to keep the rate of inflation within certain limits in order to ensure price stability. Any expansion that exceeds the limits of what is possible should be abandoned. Before driving a larger, yet unsafe, business home, you could first agree on a smaller contract on favorable terms.

The ability to consolidate a variety of information sources into an integrated view with spark innovative ideas for an ongoing adaptation to changes in the markets is key for success. Each successful enterprise has established its core values and competencies to guide their employees and drive its operations. At *Adidas*, it's all about achieving peak performance with the aim "*to be the best sports company in the world.*" With a clear understanding that there is always more information out there, *Google* is known to "*do the right thing*" via user centricity. IKEA is known for focusing on being long-lasting through cost-conscious *simplicity* in creating functional home furnishing products. They all surely win with persistence of the long-term vision as broadly outlined in the verse 78 of TTC

> *Water is the softest and most yielding substance.*
> *Yet nothing is better than water,*
> *for overcoming the hard and rigid,*
> *because nothing can compete with it.*
> *Everyone knows that the soft and yielding*
> *overcomes the rigid and hard,*
> *but few can put this knowledge into practice.*
> *Therefore, the Master says:*
> *"Only he who is the lowest servant of the kingdom,*
> *is worthy to become its ruler.*
> *He who is willing tackle the most unpleasant tasks,*
> *is the best ruler in the world."*
> *True sayings seem contradictory.*

The fluid nature of water as a metaphor is unmatched in embodying the unity of opposites and their connectivity. Adapting to the environment, it demonstrates tremendous strength. Only a principal, able to accept personal responsibility for misfortune in her assigned domain, is worthy of leading sustainably. Personality, tolerance, and gentle persistence will always prevail obstacles with the resolute and perseverance.

A centralized corporate office needs to establish integrating mechanisms. To serve customers in the best-possible way, the superseding strategy shall pay attention to a proper escalation policy.

> At my latest employer, the "Strategic Customer Program" (SCP) could operate from the executive level down to the engineers in the services and support organization. Qualified global accounts could be handled from a corporate perspective, supporting regional and business area management. Selection criteria for the designated companies go beyond potential revenue and profit to a strategic relevance across regions. The SCP Champion had to provide a 360-degree customer view to the executive sponsor, who was personally assigned as an escalation point for at least two years. His duty was constant review of changes in customer's business position within that industry. In close contact with the responsible account management and services organizations, it included tracking comprehensive views within the own company as well as any interference with competition, providing up-to-date and accurate information. These views aided regular meetings with the customer representatives, securing a reduction in escalation errands.

From the headquarters points of view, the driving force for selection of optimal location is overall economic benefits. To sustain effective leadership, one needs proper understanding of how to apply location economies by utilizing benefits from value creation in the best fitting region taking into consideration market dynamics, an enhanced product quality, resource availability, and any further factor endowments. Rewarding skills can appear anywhere within global operations.

Agile organizations rely on a scalable network of empowered and cohesive teams. The truly adaptive enterprise puts customer success into a key part of everyone's role—from marketing and sales through to service and support. Repeatedly, fruitful partnerships are needed with a responsible leadership by empowerment to cover the whole range of required functions, such as research and development, production, trade, customer services, and support. By these means, developing an understanding of team effort is key, as it has been partially expressed within the verse 39 of TTC

*The Master views the parts with compassion,
because he understands the whole.*

Sustainable development is rooted in dynamic processes of open systems. Great achievements emerge from cooperation, independence can only be achieved by consideration of influencing parties.

> Accelerating global integration, one of the largest electronics companies in the world has initiated SPEED (Superior Production Execution through ERP Deployment) program. In the preparation for business transformation, knowledge of expertise teams in the engineering center in Europe has been combined with input from leading consulting companies. Under the leadership and coordination from HQ in Europe, methodological reviews with representatives from entities in the US and Asia Pacific have been conducted. Several topical workshops ensured alignment of the company staff with suppliers around common targets with shared values towards commitment in the fulfillment of such a large-scale change program within envisioned milestones. A globally respectable competence development initiative for vendor neutral and implementation independent applications has been established. Implementation teams were mainly engaged from their India operations, bringing experiences in global distributed software development. Testing efforts were concerted in the Latin American hubs. Revised and proven building blocks could be rolled-out with assistance of their support organizations in Asia–Pacific. The global approach took iterations, yet could progress according to envisioned goals.

Within international business, *decentralization* is a necessary component of expansion into new geographical areas. It contributes to higher flexibility in the utilization of resources. Flexible transnational strategy shall consider responsiveness to different local conditions in relation to effectivity of global value-chain objectives. Optimization of economic factors opens to new areas through flexible options for reliability based on the division of labor. To illustrate this point, let us review an example of the organizational benefits that result from adoption to scalability demands in services across markets.

> In the past, our *Services* organization used to be managed mainly driven by the needs at local and regional levels. Following increased globalization pressures, it was required to establish solid global structures for the implementation of industrial, business, and technological solutions. Top management has decided that customer-facing roles (such as, solution architects and project managers) shall remain in the local structures. All business and application consultants were then concentrated in the central delivery division, to be engaged where they are needed. An agile quarterly re-planning of the workforce demand based on the current agreements and foreseen pipeline was established. Due to the successful realization, some parts of the support organization have also been included, resulting in the overall optimization in customer care.

More than ever, it is important to pay attention to the people who can gain an overview of key trends. Success lies in the attention to detail but flexibility in execution. The culminating point of achievement on the evolving way is emphasizing everlasting attributes of sage leaders in the final verse 81 in TTC

> *Knowers do not generalize,*
> *generalists do not know.*
> *Sages do not accumulate anything*
> *but give everything to others,*
> *having more the more they give.*

While the value chains are getting even longer, moderating roles of exemplary leaders are securing favorable linkages within transition to the sustainable development goals. Supply chain resilience is also playing an increasingly important role in the global marketplace. Awareness of balancing in taking and giving is a foundation of true value-based relationships.

Any business within emerging markets requires a flexible but well-structured and managed framework around articulated objectives. By entering an emerging market, it might be beneficial to get a trusted intermediary, either of local origin or with established connections, able to facilitate relevant meetings to assist in the resolution of differences. The proper mix of diverse resources and capabilities will enable partners to create value in flexible utilization in many ways. It pays off to be compassionate in providing an extraordinary service. Kouzes and Posner enlist in Practice 4 *"when people take personal responsibility and are held accountable for their actions, their colleagues are much more inclined to want to work with them and are more motivated to cooperate in general."* (Kouzes and Posner 2012).

With this treatise, we have reviewed several key attributions of leadership and their attributes in relation to management practices. Comparatively, they have been put into a juxtaposition to Taoist verses in TTC that primarily illustrate the natural tendency to grasp the genuine circumstance and take a likely route in line with fundamental principles. As an actual matter, to endure diverse business challenges and ensure positive results, hybrid forms of leadership and management require flexibility in continuous adaptation to ongoing changes.

Without any further ado, be encouraged to reflect how statements in the verses of *Tao Te Ching* transmit to present-day business life.

Appendix

It shows courage to revise the established ideas and to break new ground. While managers are guided by existing rules, leaders are always ready to open themselves to new insights that come from well-informed sources. As a great visionary, Tim Berners-Lee has developed the *World Wide Web* in 1991, yet it was only in the years that followed that Marc Andreessen made a decisive contribution to the *information revolution* with the introduction of easy-to-use browsers.

Most aspects of leadership are "*not rocket science*," yet many business leaders still have little understanding of the application of sustainable, extraordinary methods. Particularly, when exploiting an emerging market, there are pressing challenges to be addressed, and Taoist views provide valuable insights for advancements in matching vivid perspectives with ongoing business questions. Who shall become the prime target? What are their pressing needs? Which of the evolving opportunities can be addressed with capabilities at hand? How to establish a mutually beneficial relationship? When are expected benefits going to occur? Quite often, it is about the ability to recognize promising regularities from recurring patterns of success. For a truly successful commercialization, one's own interests should also be able to relate to general societal needs. A strategist uses the insights gained to integrate the interests of different customer groups in the sales markets with comprehensive offers.

Any attempts to tempt interpretations within this treatise are meant to reveal the reader's mind for deeper exploration into subtle meanings of the eternal Taoist worldview. In a shift from conquering to contributing, the insights laid out by TTC can be subjected to further empirical refinement. We live in great times to perform something meaningful that can reach beyond satisfaction of immediate needs.

There are principles that apply to all branches of a globally active company in the sense of a *"corporate citizen."* One cannot ask the questions about the overriding goals and objectives often enough. By challenging any conventional wisdom, when you know the right things to do, just consider how to make them right. All that can be said for sure is that the ancient wisdom of Taoism is further on offering value to Western Hemisphere executives in the appreciation of timeless values relating to today's leadership styles. The more you contemplate the verses from TTC, the more they reveal everlasting principles of true leadership that conform to the ideals of classical Taoism and appreciate hints on managing business on the journey to a rewarding lifestyle.

There is no shortcut to lifelong recognition of underlying reality (*TAO*) that is continuously presented in numerous virtues (*TE*). Thinking of Taoism as a master virtue enables individuals, organizations, and society to cultivate a sense of sustainable living. It's true that all virtues are derived from fundamental principles, as it has been expressed in the verse 70 of TTC

> *My sayings are very easy to recognize, and very easy to apply.*
> *But no one in the world can recognize them,*
> *and no one can apply them.*
> *Sayings have a source, events have a leader.*
> *It is only through ignorance that I am not known.*
> *Those who know me are rare; those who emulate me are noble.*
> *This is why sages dress plainly and conceal what is precious.*

A passed-down wisdom can well lay behind an unexceptional appearance. Open-minded leaders look beyond obvious externals by embracing various possibilities upon uncommon perspectives or suggestions. Following the taken course, they modestly avoid flaunting gained positions respective achieved accomplishments by appreciating contributions of their pendants.

With attained understanding of Taoist considerations, let's match an illustrative example of GOSPA terms to TTC verses (in bracket):

> *Goal*: gain excellence in adherence to fundamental principles (38);
> yield to changes through competence and cooperation (8)
> *Objective*: execute cultivation of harmonious relationships (54);
> continuously warrant wide-ranging knowledge base (21)
> *Strategy*: succeed with marginal steps in the natural course (63);
> deliberately obey the precautionary principle (64);
> perform continuous learning as conditions unfold (48)
> *Plan*: pursue utilization of evolving circumstances (57);
> deploy refined iterations within circular development (44)
> *Action*: ascertain principles for efficient operating methods (81);
> considerate balance of resistance with self-efficacy (43);
> attain balance through attentive moderation (59)

To draw valid conclusions on the key insights being emphasized with the reference to approaches rooted in Taoism, let's review a short overview of Taoist approach with derived practices for managerial implications, and table certain leadership aspects as well as related managerial competences.

Taoist Approach

The twofold coverage of distinct characteristics somewhat presents deliberate examination, notwithstanding that some features might overlay within single personality traits. Overlapping leadership and management acts can converge in the review of the possibility and feasibility when leaders get to think big and make bold decisions, while managers effectively subscribe to current business positions.

A substantial matter could be disturbed by restless interference with the natural flow of the ongoing processes. Ultimately, we can ponder on the principle of non-interference with the natural flow of the ongoing processes. Many value-added activities are inextricably linked with each other toward a harmonious relationship, as partly outlined below. With its current spread around the world, Taoism prevails in adopting cultural meanings.

Situation	Conventional behavior	Taoist approach
Ongoing steady appearances	Establishment of the elevated circulation dynamics in the business conduct	Considerations from cyclical tendencies
Facing ongoing contradictions	Fostering persuasion based on achieved positions	Alignment of contrasting polarities
Severe change in conditions	Applying change management within established business processes	Adaptive enterprise with agile methods
Unanticipated downturns	Reversion in the strategy or taken direction	Stabilization of fair value estimates

Leadership Appearance

Leadership is a responsible task. A distinct leadership quality can be seen as a rare energy (*yang*) applied to balance critical considerations.

Certain genuine attributions play a conclusive role in several verses of the TTC, as outlined below.

Leadership	Selected quote from TTC verse	Meaning
Vital and viable efforts	"Its vitality is very genuine Within it we can find order." (21)	Non-coercive actions
Performing effortless actions	"The sage discards the extremes, the extravagant and the excessive" (29)	Applying non-interference
Dialectical unity of opposites	"The soft overcomes the hard The slow overcomes the fast Let your workings remain a mystery. Just show people the results." (36)	Dynamic integration of contrasting states
Contrasting thinking	"Gravity is the root of lightness; calm is the master of excitement." (26)	Goals for the greater good
Best efficacy from collaboration	"Master is willing to help everyone and doesn't know the meaning of rejection." (27)	Alignment on shared targets

(continued)

(continued)

Leadership	Selected quote from TTC verse	Meaning
Considerations of the wellbeing	*"When sages ... want to precede people, they go after them in status."* (66)	Distinct quality of selflessness in persuasion

Managerial Implications

We can also match an attribution of substantial (*yin*) skills within the extraordinary managerial competences.

Skills	Selected TTC verses	Competence
Deliberate avoidance of domination	*"Because he believes in himself, he doesn't try to convince others..."* (30), see also verses 2, 7, 54	Courage to *"let it be"* following the main course of the strategic development
Reverse thinking in practical problem solving	*"If you know when to stop, you'll suffer no harm."* (44), see also verses 3, 9, 11, 81	Considerations of root causes by changing little lead for significant impact
Awareness of reality	*"He dwells in reality, and lets all illusions go."* (21), see 12, 63, 70	Understanding of the natural developments
Governance without interruptions	*"In governing, don't try to control."* (8), see also verses 30, 60	Rejection of upsetting manipulative actions
Care in integration	*"Diminish the self and curb the desires"* (19), see also the verses 4, 5, 13, 49, 66, 74	Deliberation of natural environment and comfort of players
Cultivation of enduring relationships	*"The Master doesn't try to be powerful; thus he is truly powerful."* (38), see also the verses 10, 29, 49, 54, 60, 61	Set up and ongoing maintenance of the tenable development

Selected Sources

The following books belong to the business executive's bookshelf.

Buffett, Mary & Clark, David (2008). The Tao of Warren Buffett. Pocket Books.

Chandler, Steve (2005). The Joy of Selling. Robert D. Reed Publishers.

Chemers, Martin M. (1997). An integrative theory of leadership. Lawrence Erlbaum Associates.

Clarke, J.J. (2000). The Tao of the West: *Western Transformations of Taoist Thought*. Routledge.

Gerstner, Ansgar (2010). The Tao of Business: *Using Ancient Chinese Philosophy to Survive and Prosper in Times of Crisis*. Earnshaw Books.

Goleman, Daniel (2013). "Primal Leadership: *Unleashing the power of emotional intelligence*", Harvard Business Review Press.

Guo, Xuezhi (2019). The Politics of the Core Leader in China: *Culture, Institution, Legitimacy, and Power*. Cambridge University Press.

Heider, John (2015). The Tao of Leadership: *Lao Tzu's Tao Te Ching Adapted for a New Age*. Greed Dragon Books.

Khanna, Parag (2019). The Future is Asian: *Global Order in the 21st Century*. Weidenfeld & Nicolson.

Kouzes, James M. and Posner, Barry Z. (2012). The Leadership Challenge *How to Make Extraordinary Things Happen in Organizations*. Jossey-Bass A Wiley Imprint.

Landsberg, Max (2015). The Tao of Coaching. Profile Books.

Related Websites

- The Tao of Business Success: Balancing *yin* and *yang* strategies (www.1000ventures.com/business_guide/tao_business.html)
- Taoism views (www.sciencedirect.com/topics/social-sciences/taoism)
- Commentary overview of Lǎozǐ Dàodéjīng (www.tao-te-king.org)
- Daoist leadership: theory and application by Yueh-Ting Lee, Ai-Guo Han, Tammy K. Byron, Hong-Xia Fan (pp. 83–107 as Chap. 3

in the "Leadership and Management in China", Cambridge University Press) (www.indigenouspsych.org/Interest%20Group/Lee/Daoist leadershiptheory9780521879613c03_p83-107.pdf)
- Understanding Taoist leadership from the Western perspective (pp. 47–52 in Journal of Business, 1(2), 2012 ISSN:2233-369X) (https://jb.ibsu.edu.ge/jms/index.php/jb/article/view/43/51)
- The Tao of complex adaptive systems (2011) by Man Joe Ma, A. and Osula, B. in *Chinese Management Studies* Vol. 5 No. 1, pp. 94–110 (www.doi.org/10.1108/17506141111118480)
- How Daoism can make a difference in business. (2017, April 27) blog by Helena Viera (https://blogs.lse.ac.uk/businessreview/2017/04/27/how-daoism-can-make-a-difference-in-business/)
- Liangrong, Zu (2019) Purpose-driven leadership for sustainable business: *From the Perspective of Taoism*. Retrieved December 3, 2022, from https://jcsr.springeropen.com/articles/10.1186/s40991-019-0041-z
- Helmers, Patrick. The Tao Te Ching of Sales: Universal Principles for Selling Professionals (https://www.taotechingofsales.com)
- Buffett, Warren (2010). Talks to MBA Students (www.youtube.com/watch?v=SsWUWtKsajA)

GPSR Compliance

The European Union's (EU) General Product Safety Regulation (GPSR) is a set of rules that requires consumer products to be safe and our obligations to ensure this.

If you have any concerns about our products, you can contact us on

ProductSafety@springernature.com

In case Publisher is established outside the EU, the EU authorized representative is:

Springer Nature Customer Service Center GmbH
Europaplatz 3
69115 Heidelberg, Germany

www.ingramcontent.com/pod-product-compliance
Lightning Source LLC
LaVergne TN
LVHW041204250326
834689LV00001BA/6